The Change Handbook

First Edition

The Change Handbook

First Edition

Production and Administrative Staff

Peter Burow   Concept Development, Copy Writer and Editor
Andrew James   Research and Copy Writing
Amanda Banhidi   Editor
Wade McFarlane   Desktop Publishing

First printed in 2003
Reprinted in 2004, 2006, 2007, 2012, 2014

Foreward

Dear Reader,

Welcome to this practical step-by-step guide for leaders and managers wanting to drive cultural transformation. Used well, the suggestions in this handbook will help you create teams with clear principles, a united purpose and a sense of empowerment that will drive the change your organisation so desperately wants and needs to achieve its corporate objectives.

Let's face it, in today's society, all of us are constantly facing change, in both our work and personal lives. The way we respond to and manage change impacts not only our happiness but also our careers and long-term prosperity.

As a manager, you will have encountered considerable change over the past few years. These changes have developed and evolved your organisation into the business it is today but there is still more work to be done.

As many of you know from first hand experience, irrespective of your role or the initiatives you have sought to introduce, implementing change in any organisation can be extremely difficult.

According to research conducted by the Australian Graduate School of Management within the University of New South Wales, of the 243 organisations they studied for their book *Change Power*, 67 percent said new initiatives had gone wrong and that 92 percent of managers had overestimated the organisation's ability to successfully implement change. This is because change, if not properly managed, will be met with serious antagonism, complacency, and other blocking actions.

If these problems are to be overcome, an organisation-wide and unified approach to managing change is vital. This handbook is a how-to guide to help you become a better, more effective manager who can keep your people engaged in a constantly evolving environment.

I hope you find this handbook useful. I look forward to your comments and feedback over the coming months and wish you well with the initiatives you are introducing.

Yours sincerely,

Peter Burow

September 2013

Dedication

This book is dedicated to all the leaders and teams that have had the courage to undertake this process.

Introduction

Welcome to The Change Handbook. This handbook is designed to provide managers of all backgrounds and experience with an easy-to-follow process for effectively managing change, irrespective of the specific area in which you work or the size of your team.

Based on years of academic and practical research, this Handbook seeks to explain how your projects can be introduced in a way that ensures maximum employee engagement as well as the delivery of tangible, measurable results within an acceptable timeframe.

How Best to Use This Handbook

How you choose to use this handbook will depend on how you prefer to read and absorb information. For those of you with a more academic or study- based background, you may prefer to read the Handbook from cover to cover before focussing on the chapters that deal specifically with the action you need to take to complete each phase in the process.

Alternatively, for those who prefer to review practical examples of how the process works, you may wish to focus on Chapters One to Six, which clearly explains the process of employee engagement in detail.

In preparing this Handbook, we have worked hard to ensure that each chapter provides valuable and relevant information that managers can use in their everyday roles.

At the end of each chapter we have included a checklist that details each of the steps you need to take. These checklists will not only allow you to keep your process on track but will also enable you and your team to measure the progress you are making and the results you are delivering.

It is vital that you work through each of the checklists before moving on to the next chapter. To help answer any questions or queries you may encounter along the way, we have also included some Frequently Asked Questions (FAQ's) in Chapter Seven. If you find you or your team are encountering difficulties in completing any of the six phases, please refer to these FAQ's for more help.

There are a number of ways in which you can use this Handbook. The one you choose will depend on how you prefer to read and absorb information.

- Read it cover to cover

- Use it as a reference tool with practical examples

- Read the chapters relevant to you

In preparing this Handbook, we have worked hard to ensure that each chapter provides valuable and relevant information that managers can use in their everyday roles. At the end of each chapter we have included a checklist that outlines each of the steps you need to take before you move on to the next phase.

Background to This Handbook

Over the years, there have been many books written on the subject of effective change management. Each has contributed to and helped evolve the change management process not just in Australia but around the globe. In preparing this Handbook, I have drawn information from a variety of these sources including academics, detailed research and the experience of managers from other Australian organisations.

More specifically, I have included information from the extensive research undertaken by John P Kotter from the Harvard Business School in the US. In his highly successful book 'Leading Change' he explains how many US companies have encountered major challenges including complacency and, what he describes as 'underpowered coalitions', which have undermined and derailed change of every kind.

In ensuring the practical ideas in this book are relevant here in Australia, I have drawn not only on my own experience, but also on the work of two other Australian authors, Dennis Turner and Michael Crawford, who have conducted similar research across a total of 243 Australian organisations.

My professional experience in this area has been as an implementer of change in Sydney, Perth and Brisbane with organisations as large as PricewaterhouseCoopers, Suncorp, AMP, BHP Billiton Queensland Rail, GIO, Rail Infrastructure Corporation and Forest Products Commission and as small as 10-person service firms and retail outlets. In this capacity I have worked with Boards, Executive Team, HR teams, line managers, unions and literally thousands of employees to execute significant change in a way that is meaningful, practical and rewarding.

This Handbook has been written to capture the experience of all these authors and translate it into a simple step-by-step guide that converts insight into practical action.

Why Read This Handbook?

Change in any organisation is difficult. As human beings we generally do not respond well to change and can react negatively and even aggressively to changes we don't understand and therefore don't want.

As an organisation you may be committed to constantly evolving and developing the services you provide but the only way you can do this is through constant customer-focused change.

I have developed this Handbook to help you implement change in the specific areas in which you work. This Handbook explains in detail the best way to ensure everyone involved in your project embraces the change. It is designed to help you put this process into action, simply and effectively.

More than just a theory-based approach, the aim of this Handbook is to help you and your teams understand and embrace effective change management and employee engagement in a practical and grounded way.

It also gives you a simple guide to each of the phases of change, highlighting along the way the various tasks you need to complete in order to successfully deliver sustainable improvements to your organisation.

The Benefits This Handbook Will Deliver

The aim of this handbook is to:

- Ensure you succeed when introducing and implementing projects by providing you with a process that is based on a well researched, proven methodology that has been successfully actioned in other organisations throughout Australia and around the world.

- Identify each task that has to be completed before you and your team can move onto the next phase of the engagement process. This approach ensures you and your team know where more work has to be done and what comes next in the change management process.

- Make it easier to implement your project by providing a well defined, practical, powerful but simple framework for effectively managing change. We have also included additional information for those managers who may find themselves in unfamiliar territory when considering change management and want some background reading.

By taking the time to read, embrace and implement this process, you can look forward to:

- The satisfaction of introducing change or a specific project that works and delivers results, no only in the short term but also into the future. You will leave a legacy.

- Increased recognition of your work. Being able to succesfully introduce a project or some form of lasting change within an organisation is the mark of a good manager.

- Contributing to and helping establish an organisation-wide and unified approach to managing change within your organisation.

Table of Contents

Chapter 4   59

Chapter 5   73

Overview – Engagement Process

The engagement process* has six sequential phases with specific activity that needs to be undertaken in each phase. An overview of these phases is given below. Each phase focuses on:

Phase 1

Establishing a sense of urgency for introducing your project and creating a guiding coalition team with representatives of those you are encouraging to embrace the change.

Phase 2

How you develop a vision and a strategy for the project.

Phase 3

How you communicate your strategy and engage your team.

Phase 4

How you motivate your team to undertake broad-based actions and deliver short-term wins.

Phase 5

Consolidating the gains you have made and generating even more change.

Phase 6

Celebrating the project's success and gives you suggestions on ways to embed and anchor the changes you have achieved in the corporate culture of the organisation to ensure these changes endure.

Key Topics Covered in this Chapter

In this Chapter you will explore:

* The Engagement Process

* The Levers you Need to Motivate and Engage Your Team

* What engagement looks like

* For more information on the engagement process see page 6

Overview – Engagement Process

To help explain each of these phases, we have included a separate section on each of the following:

- An introduction to the phase being covered

- Key topics covered in the chapter

- Leadership style to be adopted in each phase

- Practical exercises where possible

- Tips on the DO's and DONT's of each phase

- Framework for developing your key messages for each phase

- A best guess self-assessment

- A checklist for each phase

The Nine Levers You Need to Motivate Your Team

An important key to engagement is understanding what motivates employees to embrace or resist change. As part of the research undertaken by Stanford University in the US, these various motivating factors have been grouped into nine levers of cultural change.

As part of its extensive research, Stanford University found that in any organisation, irrespective of the specific work culture, leveraging from these nine key areas is absolutely critical if change is to gain the momentum needed and be embraced long-term.

At each phase of the engagement process, these nine levers need to be considered and worked into the key messages given and the action undertaken at that phase. The more of these levers you can use, the more motivated your employees will be to adopt the proposed change.

Using the Nine Levers of Change

Everyone is motivated by one or more of these nine motivators. We are all different. What motivates you will be different from how others are motivated. As a leader you need to make sure you do not assume everyone else is motivated in the same way you are and focus on just one or two of the nine motivators or levers. Instead we need to lead in a way that appeals to all nine. That is, in our proposals, plans, speeches, emails and any other communication or presentation we need to appeal to each of the nine motivators. That way we engage the greatest support for change, multiplying our chances for success.

The nine motivators have been organised into three groups: Red, Green and Blue. The motivators for Red are broadly process, clarity and integrity, whereas the three in the Blue section are broadly truth, curiosity, and rational thought. The motivators for the Green section are broadly achievement, recognition and connection with others. Each of us will respond to one motivator from each group. Ideally you will appeal to all nine motivators, but as a bare minimum, it is OK to use three of the nine motivators as long as one of the three comes from Red, another from Blue and the final one from Green.

In the following table, each of the nine motivators or levers of change is identified in the left column, while the right column articulates the key questions that must be addressed if the lever is to be used to maximum effect.

LEVERAGE AREA	KEY MESSAGE TO BE COMMUNICATED
Feeling Valued and Respected	• How is this change affecting all my team members? • How will this change improve team relationships? • Are we giving people the support they need to make the changes
Gaining Recognition	• How will we measure success? • What public recognition will we receive if we successfully implement the change? • What are our specific roles and responsibilities?
Making a Unique Contribution	• How does this initiative contribute to our organisation's core business? • How do we communicate this internally and externally? • Does the purpose of this project inspire our people?

LEVERAGE AREA	KEY MESSAGE TO BE COMMUNICATED
Striving for Technical Excellence	• What information do we need to know to make this initiative work? • What technical knowledge do we need? • Is our intelligence communicated? • Do we have the tools, IT, and equipment we need to do the job? • How does this initiative fit with our organisation's wider strategy?
Understanding Political Motivation	• What are the political reasons for this initiative? • What are the weaknesses of our strategy? • What opportunities have we created for employees to ask their questions about this initiative?
Celebrating and Innovating	• • What opportunities are out there that we are ignoring? • • Who can we align with to help us achieve our objectives? • • How can we reward creativity? • • What milestones can we celebrate?
Taking Practical Action	• How can we break through all the barriers and achieve our objectives as a team? • What leverage do our strengths provide? • How do we get the commitment we need to work as a single focused team?
Being Listened To	• What feedback system do we have? • How are we demonstrating respect for all points of view? • Are we keeping this project in perspective?
Taking Personal Responsibility	• How does this initiative support our shared values? • What is our authority or responsibility? • What resources do we have at our disposal to complete the task? • How will we reward compliance?

What is Employee Engagement?

Employee Engagement is where employees fully immerse in their project or their work and do whatever it takes to achieve the project's objectives. To achieve employee engagement, you need both (1) a high intensity or energy, and (2) a positive emotion in your team and organisation. Conversely, a low intensity or energy and an unpleasant mood in your organisation will cause low employee engagement.

The Dynamics of Engagement*

HIGH INTESITY/ENERGY

HIGH NEGATIVE	HIGH POSITIVE
Angry	Understanding
Fearful	Commitment
Anxious	Empowerment
Defensive	Esprit de corps
Resentful	High Workloads
Shame	
LOW NEGATIVE	LOW POSITIVE
Conflict/Defeated	Relaxed
Resistance	Mellow
Depressed	Peaceful
Exhausted	Tranquil
Burned Out	Serene
Hopeless	

NEGATIVE AFFECT (Unpleasant) **POSITIVE AFFECT (Pleasant)**

LOW INTENSITY/ENERGY

*Engagement Model: Loehr & Schwartz 2003

HIGHLIGHT
Dynamics of Engagement

As the table suggests, a lack of employee engagement means having an environment of conflict, resistance and anxiety to change, a mood of depression, exhaustion, burn-out, hopelessness and a feeling of defeat.

This reduces productivity and increases staff turnover. Reaching employee engagement means having a culture of understanding, commitment, empowerment, friendship, euphoria and high workloads.

Achieving this means doing the following steps: achieving a sense of urgency, creating and communicating a vision, communicating this initiative, evaluation, project action, broad-based action and short-term wins, producing more change, and celebrating and building continuing relationships.

These actions are expanded in detail in the chapters following.

Chapter 1

PHASE 1: Instil Urgency, Form Guiding Alliance and Set Clarity and Integrity

Introduction

The task in the first phase of the engagement process is to ensure you and your team overcome the natural complacency all of us tend to have towards breaking old habits. It is also about planning the way forward, engaging the key members of your team and focusing on getting the core elements of the process right.

Of all the six phases, this is the most critical. If you don't work through the various planning tasks and overcome the challenges and opposition you will meet at the beginning, you will have significantly more work to do in the later phases of the process.

This is because, at a later date, it will be much harder to ignite urgency in people if they have been allowed to ignore the project from the outset. If the key influential employees do not become 'Engagement Representatives', working with you towards a common goal, it will be much more difficult to win them over and gain their allegiance and support once you have started implementing your particular project. And if your integrity is compromised it is almost impossible to get it back.

If you invest maximum effort in this, the first Phase of the process, you will create the foundations, clarity and respect you will need to successfully push your project forward.

Key Topics Covered in this Chapter

In this Chapter you will explore:

- The Importance of Creating Urgency

- Ways of Forming a Powerful Guiding Alliance with your workforce

- The Importance of Clarity

- The Importance of Demonstrating Leadership Integrity

Chapter 1

PHASE 1	PHASE 2	PHASE 3	PHASE 4	PHASE 5	PHASE 6
Instil Urgency, form Guiding Alliances and Set Clarity and Integrity	Develop Vision and Strategy	Engage the team and communicate the stratey.	Get broad-based actions and short-term wins	Consolidate gains and more change	Close with a celebration

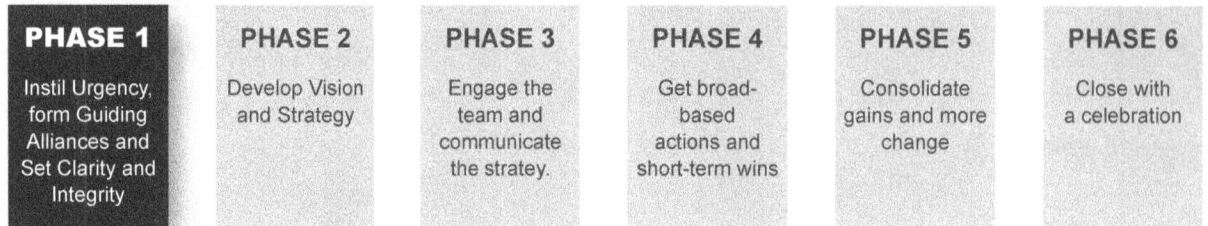

Getting Started

Phase 1 has four elements:

1. Urgency

2. Creating a Guiding Alliance

3. Clarity, and

4. Integrity

Quadrant I – Urgency

Why Do We Need Urgency?

People tend to be naturally complacent about change and often resistant to it. Even if people see a project as being constructive, there is no guarantee that they will accept or embrace it, given their natural resistance to change.

To overcome this, according to John P Kotter's extensive research, managers have to create a sense of urgency by implementing five key steps:

5. Explain the benefits of your project – for the individual members of the group, the team as a whole, the broader organisation and its stakeholders (if relevant).

The Four Elements of Phase 1

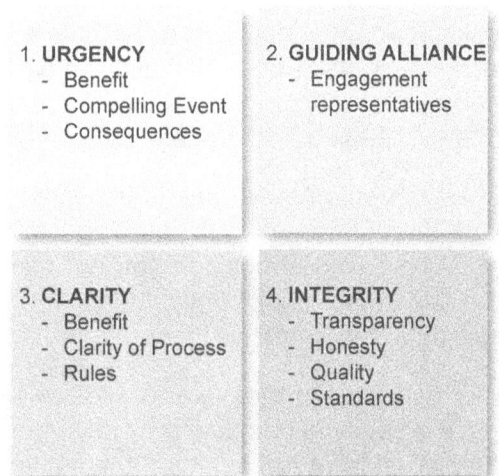

1. URGENCY
- Benefit
- Compelling Event
- Consequences

2. GUIDING ALLIANCE
- Engagement representatives

3. CLARITY
- Benefit
- Clarity of Process
- Rules

4. INTEGRITY
- Transparency
- Honesty
- Quality
- Standards

Quadrant I – Urgency

6. Create a compelling event – this needs to be an event that, in some way, is integral to or even dependent on the specific project. This event will allow you to indirectly set a deadline. Such events include:

    • The introduction of legislation

    • The next Board meeting

    • A government review

    • The budgeting cycle

    • Worker or customer safety

7. Emphasise the Rewards – for the individual members, the team as a whole and even the broader company if employees adopt the change and help drive through the implementation of your initiative.

8. Highlight the consequences of NOT implementing the project – explain the downside of the team not embracing change and not changing their behaviour to support your project. Such consequences could be potential legal action, missed opportunities or even downsizing of the team or company as a whole.

9. Immediately align your resources with the objective of the project – if, for example, the project uses budget cuts as a reason for urgency then other activities need to be in alignment with this such as the removal of extravagant executive perks, overseas travel, and other savings that can be implemented at the top to set an example to the employees as a whole. Conversely if the initiative is aimed at increased efficiency and additional resources are required for equipment and training, state the size of the budget and don't scrimp in such a way that it actually reduces efficiency.

Actions to Create Urgency

• Remove sources of complacency or minimise their impact by:

• Explaining the benefits of your project

• Leveraging a compelling event

• Highlighting the consequences of not implementing the project

• Emphasising the rewards for the team in return for compliance

• Aligning your resources with the project

Chapter 1

Leadership Style - Phase 1

Your Communication Style

- Polite
- Direct
- Responsible

Your Focus of Attention

- Always keeps sensitive information that has been shared in confidence to themselves
- Acts ethically in his/her dealings with others
- Spends time to make sure there is agreement about roles - theirs and others
- Corrects others - clearly, constructively and professionally
- Speaks directly to the person they have an issue with without unnecessarily involving other unrelated people
- Provides other team members with a sense of purpose

Key Questions

- Do we all understand the problem that we're trying to solve here?
- Is this group focusing where it should be, or are we getting off track?
- What would lead to a fair and equitable outcome for all parties?
- How can we maintain integrity as a leadership team?
- Is everyone delivering on the promises that they've made?

Your Deliverables

- Standards
- Rules
- Clear process

A Practical Example

Situation Analysis

Mr B is the manager of a maintenance team within a logistics company who has been actively involved in identifying a need for more effective machinery to replace old equipment that is more than 25 years old. The capital expenditure investment has now been approved and the new equipment has been ordered for use by the organisation as a whole.

A couple of other teams around the state have already received their new equipment but have encountered a few teething problems which Mr B's team is very aware of. As a result, there is a considerable amount of resistance to the proposed new equipment despite the constant breakdown problems Mr B and his team have on a daily basis because of the age and state of their current dated equipment.

The main reasons why the team is resisting change is because they are familiar with the current system, and are nervous about the new equipment and having to learn new maintenance techniques. They also have concerns about their own abilities to master the new machinery and are fearful that the faster, more efficient equipment may result in the team being downsized.

An Effective Solution to Phase 1 of Employee Engagement

To overcome these problems, Mr B created a sense of urgency about the new equipment by explaining the benefits the new machinery would deliver, including increased safety levels and productivity, not just for his team but for the organisation as a whole. He did this through a combination of one-on-one and team briefings as well as providing the team with photos and technical specifications for the new machinery.

Mr B also created an indirect timeframe for his team to accept and embrace change by leveraging off two compelling events. The first was a legal deadline, that is, a three month deadline by which the organisation had to sign lease agreements for the new equipment.

The second was the need for Mr B and his team to provide a briefing paper to the organisation's CEO outlining how the new machinery was being used together with a review of its performance during the first month of use. Mr B emphasised that direct input from all of Mr B's team was needed if the report was to be completed and delivered on time. This approach from Mr B ensured that the team developed a sense of urgency regarding the project and the first phase of engagement was successfully completed.

QUADRANT II: Guiding Alliance (Engagement Representative Team)

What are Engagement Representatives and Why do you Need Them?

If you are to effectively implement a project, you must have practical knowledge about how to introduce change within the team. You must also have the right employee connections to ensure the team as a whole embraces the proposed changes.

According to John P Kotter's research, these connections are not just about having the ear of the company Chief Executive Officer or a senior manager with considerable influence. Rather, it is about building a small team of representatives who can talk to, listen to and influence the wider team members at each phase and help drive through the proposed changes.

Within the engagement process, these representatives are called the 'Guiding Alliance' or the 'Engagement Representative' team whose role is twofold. Firstly to pass on to you honest, open feedback from the other employees about the way the project is travelling and secondly to constantly support the project to ensure it is successfully implemented. They are the communication bridge between the workers and the implementation team.

What Makes a Good Engagement Representative?

If a 'Guiding Alliance' is to work effectively, it must comprise the right kind of 'Engagement Representatives'. According to John P Kotter's research, those people who are invited to be part of the 'Guiding Alliance' must have:

1. **Positional power** – sufficient mainstream managers with a clear understanding about how the organisation works, at both a management and field level. This will ensure that the rest of the team cannot easily block or prevent the changes from being introduced.

2. **Expertise** – enough expertise across the different points of view to ensure that informed and intelligent decisions can be made. This expertise will not necessarily relate directly to work but may also cover issues such as discipline, work experience and nationality as well as industrial relations, in particular existing links to relevant union groups.

3. **Credibility** – to have any influence on their work colleagues and ensure they are listened to and taken seriously, the 'Engagement Representatives' must be credible, believable and trustworthy.

4. **Leadership** – a coalition of poor leaders will never succeed. Proven leaders are those who can drive through and lead the change process. They are the ones others turn to for advice and support during times of change.

QUADRANT II: Guiding Alliance (Engagement Representative Team) (cont)

How Does an Engagement Representative Team Work?

The 'Engagement Representative' team has a key role to play in every single Phase of the engagement process. A key part of this role is to attend regular team meetings, in the first instance to help define the urgency of the situation and to develop some clarity and integrity around the changes that are being proposed.

At these meetings, the team will also review the tasks that have to be completed for each Phase of the process, as listed in this Handbook, and sign them off as and when they are completed. Those milestone tasks that are yet to be completed must be duly noted and addressed at the next meeting. The team cannot move on to the next Phase until all the milestone tasks have been confirmed as completed.

Later in the process, the team will also be responsible for reviewing the changes that have been implemented and for clarifying additional changes that may need to be implemented.

Outside of these regular meetings, the 'Engagement Representative' team will act as 'Advocates for Change', delivering positive key messages about the proposed project, explaining and highlighting the benefits it will deliver, the rewards the team can look forward to if they adopt the change, and the consequences the team may face if they choose to block or resist change.

How do you Create an Engagement Representative Team?

Step 5.　Be clear about the number of people who will be affected by the changes you are proposing. Of these people, you only need between five to ten per cent to become Engagement Representatives. This means if the change will affect 47 employees, you will only need between two and four 'Engagement Representatives' to help you drive through your proposed initiative.

Step 6.　Be clear about the various departments and groups that will be affected by your proposed changes. Make sure you take into account all geographical locations, functional areas such as human resources, specific task groups, unions and even external parties such as associations or professional representative bodies. Having done this, you then need to identify those people who have the respect and trust of their colleagues and who can exert real influence over those with whom they work.

Step 7.　Having identified the people you want, you now need to confirm their willingness to take on the role. Before talking to them directly, you may need to contact their immediate manager to ensure they are comfortable for that person to become an 'Engagement Representative' in the project.

QUADRANT II: Guiding Alliance (Engagement Representative Team) (cont)

Step 8. Having gained the co-operation of their managers, you then need to contact the person directly, either in person, by email or letter, to explain why you want them to be an 'Engagement Representative' and what the role will entail.

Step 9. You now need to draw together your overall strategy and detailed plan of implementation for change. As part of this process, you will need to consult your new Engagement Representatives by asking for their input and feedback on your proposed strategy and plan.

Step 10. By getting these people to work together as a group, you will create the mutual understanding and enthusiasm that is needed to lead change and successfully cut through the complacency and resistance you will inevitably encounter.

QUADRANT III: Clarity

What are the Benefits of Creating Clarity?

You cannot expect people to do what they do not understand or what is not clear to them. If you want them to embrace your project and the resulting changes, you must clearly specify what you are proposing and what impact your project will have.

What is Clarity?

Clarity is achieved by:

11. **Saying it like it is** – in an environment of change, it is essential that managers speak honestly and openly. For example, if the changes you are proposing will have a negative impact in some way it is important to say exactly that. Do not try to hide the bad news, even if there is a risk some team members will react negatively or aggressively to what you are telling them. Say it like it is at the beginning of the process rather than having team members discover the truth half way down the track.

12. **Explaining the rules** – do not be afraid to spell out the rules of behaviour that apply during and after the period of change. Be open when answering questions about whether the rules have changed and what is expected of each team member during and after the project has been implemented.

13. **Being clear about what standards and quality levels apply** – deal directly with the team's questions about what new standards, if any, they will be expected to meet and what levels of quality will now be required.

14. **Explaining what is expected of people** – brief your team, clearly and simply, about what is actually expected of them and what they will have to achieve. You will also need to make it clear whether what you expected of them previously still applies.

The DO's and DONT's for Achieving Clarity

Do

✓ State what is in it for them to embrace the change and the clear consequences of not embracing the change.

✓ State the facts, quantify them and make it relevant and practical to your audience - Say it like it is.

✓ Communicate clearly what areas will not change.

Don't

✗ Ignore bad news and pretend it is not there.

✗ Make it too high-level, academic or irrelevant to the workers or team members.

✗ Only tell your team what they want to hear.

Chapter 1

QUADRANT III: Clarity (cont)

15. **Not avoiding money issues** – be upfront about the financial impact of the changes you are proposing and provide as much information as you can in response to questions such as 'how much will we be paid for this? And if their financial rewards are to remain the same then say so.

16. **Outlining what resources are needed** – make sure you explain whether any additional employees or other resources are necessary for your project to be implemented. Make sure you are clear in your own mind what the top six roles are in your project and whether you have the right people to fill these roles.

17. **Providing clear job descriptions** – to be an effective manager, you must provide the information that every employee will want to know when faced with change, that is, how the project will affect their personal role or job description.

18. **Implementing two-way communication** – you will not achieve clarity by talking at or 'telling' your team to force them to accept the changes you are proposing. Clarity can only be achieved by allowing people to freely contribute their ideas and by drawing on the thoughts and opinions of other members of the team, not just your own.

19. **Developing a project briefing sheet** – this includes a description of what the project is, why it is being done, who is involved, when it will be started and finished and how it will be implemented.

QUADRANT IV: Integrity

What are the Benefits of Integrity?

Acting with integrity provides managers with the respect they need to drive a project forward. Conversely, managers who lack integrity create suspicion and cynicism.

What is Integrity?

Acting with integrity means:

20. **Adhering to your corporate values** – as a manager you need to ensure you strictly adhere to the six corporate values of People, Results, Integrity, Developing, Effective/Efficient and Pride. (For more information about each of these values, please see Appendix C).

21. **Being honest and trustworthy** – in return, team members will feel comfortable and safe enough to reveal their true and real feelings to you.

22. **Being courteous to people** – this will encourage your team to discuss their problems with you and seek your help to overcome these problems.

23. **Acting fairly and justly** – make sure your project is perceived as being fair and is not seen as unjust to a particular person or group of people including other employees, management, colleagues or clients.

24. **Believing in what you are doing** – if you say you are going to promote employees or provide pay increases to encourage people to embrace your project, you had better be prepared to deliver on your promises. If you cannot meet these promises, do not make them.

25. **Acting professionally** – it is vital managers are honest with their teams. If there are problems to be overcome, as part of the change process, you cannot sweep them under the carpet. If you do, your project will fail because it will not be a true representation of what you are trying to do.

Chapter 1

QUADRANT IV: Integrity (cont)

Actions to Improve Clarity and Integrity

If necessary, adjust the job descriptions of your team members. Ensure all job descriptions are aligned with the objectives of your project. If you adjust a job description you may also need to get someone from:

- Human Resources (HR) to clarify the implications of your project, particularly from a 'Union' point of view. HR input will help ensure your project is not blocked as a result of issues such as workplace health and safety or industrial relations.

- Legal to confirm that your project is legally appropriate .

- Accounts to review the budgetary implications of your project. The spending requirement for your project needs to be affordable and within budget.

- Marketing or Public Relations to review the brand and public image/perception implications of your project. The public image/perception of your project will need to be congruent with the organisation as a whole.

- Set higher standards – both formally, in the planning process, and informally in your day-to-day interaction with your team. For example, set productivity levels, customer satisfaction standards and cycle-time targets so high that they cannot be reached through the current business approach.

- Insist more people be held accountable for broader measures of organisational performance – for example widen the performance measures for sub-units. If the previous performance measure was the transportation of 2,000 barrels daily, broaden this measure to 2,000 being transported daily but also no more than two complaints about late deliveries being received weekly or monthly.

- Change your internal measurement systems to focus on the right indices - this will have a major impact as it will ensure your measurement systems are aligned with the organisations's defined strategies.

- Significantly increase the amount of external performance feedback you provide to team members.

- Reward honest, open communication in meetings as well as team members who are willing to confront problems.

- Stop baseless happy talk from the top down - If there is bad news then tell your team what it is.

- Identify and discuss crises (including potential crises) as well as major opportunities.

Developing Your Key Messages for Phase 1

The following table provides a guide for the development of the key messages and the approach you will need to adopt during this phase. This communication can take place with formal channels including presentation, noticeboards, newsletters, emails, telephone messages or informal channels such as informal face-to-face communication and hallway conversations.

LEVERAGE AREA	KEY MESSAGE TO BE COMMUNICATED
Feeling Valued and Respected	• Communicate the reason for change. Ensure the Engagement Representative can influence people's attitude and behaviour towards the project.
Gaining Recognition	• Communicate the timeframe for the key milestones and objectives for Phase 1 & 2. • Communicate how you will recognise the contributions of stakeholders. • Communicate how the success of each Phase will be measured in terms of the overall strategy.
Making a Unique Contribution	• Communicate excellence and the importance of highest standards.
Striving for Technical Excellence	• Communicate the external events/drivers that can impact your project and create the strategic reasons for change.
Understanding Political Motivation	• Develop a presentation to explain the reasons why change is occurring from a political perspective. • Encourage Q&A's to managers, supervisors and consider a roadshow.
Celebrating and Innovating	• Outline the key project milestones and how you will celebrate the achievement of these.
Taking Practical Action	• Focus on the strengths of the project and how these will move the organisation forward. • Ensure there is complete honesty about the current situation between leaders and employees
Being Listened To	• Create a system of feedback from employees that are transparent and explain how this feedback system will work.
Taking Personal Responsibility	• Link change with responsible action. • Ensure lines of responsibility are clear.

Chapter 1

Evaluating Phase 1

Find Out What Your People Think

To evaluate the views of those affected by your initiative, you will need to talk to and make contact with approximately 20% of the employees impacted by the changes you are making. Depending on the group you are wishing to sample, you can obtain their feedback through face-to-face or telephone contact.

Before making calls, draft around six key questions you would like answered.

We have listed sample questions in the box in the margin.

Once you have contacted approximately 20% of those that are impacted by your project, you can then use the optional questionnaire (detailed on page 26) to help evaluate the

Six Sample Questions for Testing the Water

Q   Are you aware of this project?

Yes/No

Q   Is this project important to you?

Yes/No

Q   Have the benefits of the project been made clear to you?

Yes/No

Q   Are you clear about how the project will affect you?

Yes/No

Q   Do you know where you can get further information about this if you need it?

Yes/No

Best Guess Self-Assessment

progress you are making in completing Phase 1.

This questionnaire is designed to measure the sense of urgency you have created, whether your 'Engagement Representative' team is effective and whether your project has a sense of clarity and integrity. If you choose not to use the questionnaire, you will need to complete the activities highlighted in the next section.

To complete the questionnaire, please mark each question out of 10. A score of 0 means you disagree strongly with the question while a mark of 10 would mean you agree strongly with the question.

If you neither agree nor disagree with the question because you believe it is not relevant to your situation or you do not know the answer to the question then you need to give it a mark of 5.

Best Guess Survey

SECTION:	Urgency: with regard to this project	SCORE out of 10

QUESTION

1. Your team believes the current situation is unacceptable. ☐

2. Your team has a sense of urgency about the changes you are proposing. ☐

3. You have 75% of your overall management team and 90% of your top executives believing that the changes you are proposing are absolutely essential. ☐

4. Your well-informed customers, suppliers, or (if relevant) shareholders support the changes you are proposing. That is, they are not showing a high degree of complacency or resistance to the changes. ☐

5. Your people are open to your strategy for implementing the change. ☐

6. Morale and short-term performance in your team is not slipping. ☐

7. Your team does not believe that "sure we have some big problems but they are all someone else's responsibility"? Other versions of the same thing include: ☐
   a. "When they stop restructuring we'll be in great shape."
   b. "As soon as the War on Waste savings kick in, the numbers will go up."
   c. "The bigger problems are over there, my division is fine."

Total Urgency Score ☐

Best Guess Survey (cont)

SECTION:	Integrity and Clarity: with regard to this project	SCORE out of 10
	QUESTION	

1. Your communication has been effective. That is, you have talked to *and* have got feedback from other stakeholders. ☐

2. You have shared information with your team honestly. ☐

3. You have clarified everyone's role, remuneration and what is expected of them. ☐

4. You have clarified the rules, quality and standard expectations. ☐

5. Your project is just and fair to all groups including employees, management and clients. ☐

6. People are doing what they say they are doing and this includes yourself. ☐

Total Total Integrity and Clarity Score ☐

Interpreting and Plotting the Results/The Resulting Actions

If you completed the Best Guess survey you can now plot your results on the Phase 1 Self-Assessment Chart on page 28. Plot your score from the Urgency section on the X-axis and the score from the Integrity and Clarity section on the Y-axis. This tells you what quadrant you are in.

If you did not complete the Self-Assessment survey then you will need to assume you are in quadrant B.

Then, using this quadrant letter, look up the following table to clarify your recommended action.

PHASE 1 Best Guess Diagnostic

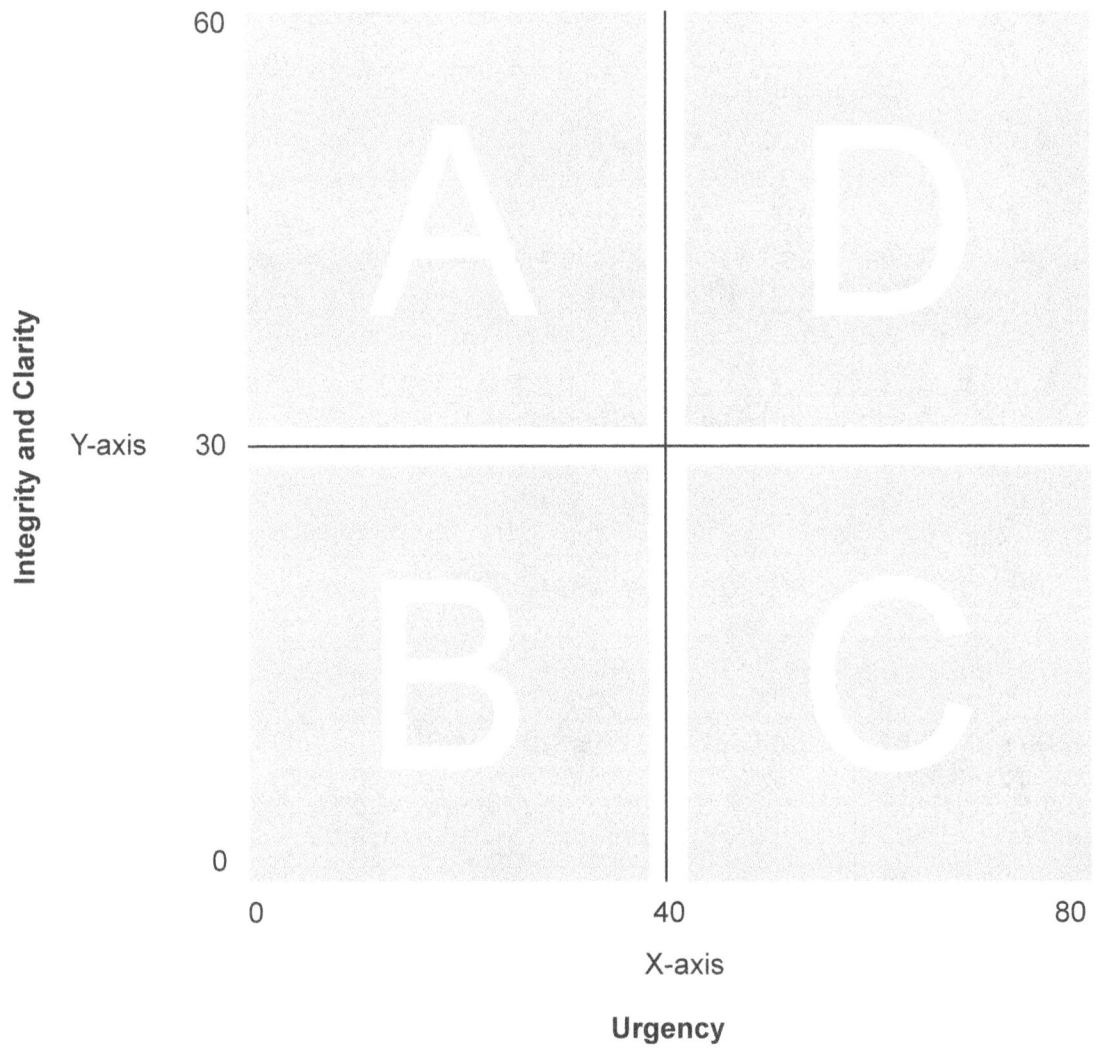

Interpreting the Results/The Resulting Actions

Quadrant	Diagnosis	Action Required
A	If you find yourself in quadrant A, you need to take further action to improve a sense of urgency.	**Remove sources of complacency or minimise their impact:** • Explain the benefits of your project. (See page 8) • Leverage from a compelling event.(See page 9) • Highlight the consequences of not implementing the project.(See page 9) • Emphasise the rewards for the team in return for compliance. (See page 9) • Align your resources with the project.
B	If you find yourself in quadrant B, you need to take further action to improve clarity and integrity as well as create a sense of urgency.	**Add clarity and integrity and remove complacency:** • Leverage from a compelling event to add urgency. • Highlight the consequences of not implementing the project. • Emphasise the rewards for the team in return for compliance. • Adjust job descriptions adding clarity where necessary. • Set higher standards. • Insist more people be held accountable for broader measures of organisational performance. • Change your internal measurement systems to focus on the right indices. • Significantly increase the amount of external performance feedback to team members. • Reward honest and open communication. • Don't withhold bad news from your team. • Identify and discuss crises, potential crises and opportunities.
C	If you find yourself in quadrant C, you need to take further action to improve clarity and integrity.	• **Add clarity and integrity by:** • Contracting key resources where necessary. • Adjusting job descriptions where necessary. • Setting higher standards. • Insisting more people be held accountable for broader measures of organisational performance. • Changing your internal measurement systems to focus on the right indices. • Significantly increasing the amount of external performance feedback to team members. • Rewarding honest and open communication. • Not withholding bad news from your team. • Identifying and discussing crises, potential crises and opportunities.
D	If you find yourself in quadrant D, you have successfully implemented Phase 1 effectively.	• You are ready to move to the next phase.

• ***After taking steps to ensure the initiative successfully completes Phase 1, repeat this self-assessment until you find yourself in quadrant D, at which point you can review the Phase 1 checklist to ensure all the necessary tasks have been completed. At this point you can move on to Phase 2.**

Chapter 1

PHASE 1 Checklist

When you can tick each item in the following checklist, you are ready to move to Phase 2.

☐ I clearly understand how the team feels about the project.

☐ I have created a sense of urgency so those involved can see why we need to implement the required changes quickly.

☐ I have clarified the key messages.

☐ I have identified and appointed the Engagement Representatives.

☐ The Engagement Representatives understand the project, why it is happening and how the strategy will be rolled out.

☐ I have contacted the HR, Legal, Accounts and Marketing/PR teams about the project.

☐ I have developed a project briefing-sheet which includes a description of what the project is, why it is being done, who is involved, when it will be started and finished and how it will be implemented.

☐ I have developed the key messages I will use based on the Nine Levers of Change.

Chapter 2

PHASE 2: Develop a Vision and Strategy

Introduction

Having completed the required activity in Phase 1, you and your team are now ready to move on to Phase 2.

The aim of Phase 2 is to provide you with the tools you need to explain the vision and strategy that underpins your project. One of the key requirements of Phase 2 is for you, as a manager, to spend time with your 'Engagement Representatives' explaining your vision and strategy so they become empowered and enthusiastic in seeking to influence the remaining members of your team and the organisation as a whole.

Phase 2 is the heart and soul of the whole engagement process. If you implement Phase 2 well, your project will gain both momentum and support. In addition, your team will find it easier to understand what you're trying to achieve and will gradually see how specific activities are all part of the changes and improvements you are trying to implement.

The advantage of Phase 2 is that more and more people within your team will start to self-manage and begin to implement positive supportive activities rather than getting bogged down with bureaucracy.

Key Topics Covered in this Chapter

In this Chapter you will explore:

- Developing and communicating your vision

- Developing and communicating your strategy.

Chapter 2

PHASE 1	PHASE 2	PHASE 3	PHASE 4	PHASE 5	PHASE 6
Instil Urgency, form Guiding Alliances and Set Clarity and Integrity	Develop Vision and Strategy	Engage the team and communicate the stratey.	Get broad-based actions and short-term wins	Consolidate gains and more change	Close with a celebration

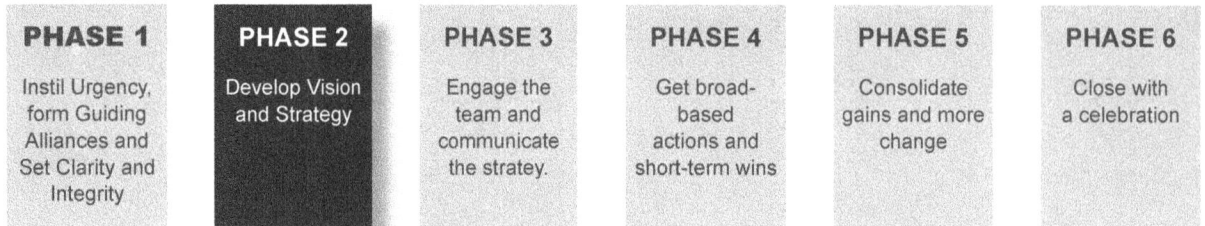

What is a Vision?

To successfully implement Phase 2, you will first need to understand what a vision is. A vision is the big picture of the future described in words. It normally includes a very brief commentary about why the organisation should strive to implement the project.

A vision also seeks to say: 'This is how our world is changing and here are some compelling reasons why we should set these goals. These are the goals and these are the benefits of achieving them.'

What is Strategy?

Having defined the project vision, you now need to understand what a strategy is. In simple terms, a strategy explains how an organisation or team is going to achieve its vision.

When formulating a strategy it is important to have a clear understanding of the organisation's operating environment, in particular the competitive trends it faces rather than basing decisions solely on internal self-analysis.

Once you have gained this understanding, you are ready to build a strategy that provides a logical and detailed plan as to how you, your team and your organisation as a whole are going to achieve the agreed vision.

Project Vision

▼

Project Strategy

▼

Project Goals

▼

Detailed Plan

Why is Vision and Strategy Essential for Implementing Your Project?

The importance of having a clear vision and strategy cannot be emphasised enough. Creating a vision is essential for implementing a project for three main reasons:

1. Clarity

   By providing clarity, you will significantly simplify the decision-making process. This is because in everything they do employees will simply have to ask themselves - is this in line with our vision?

   This simple process can be applied to major decisions such as the fit of existing projects, acquisitions or capital expenditure with an organisation's agreed vision. This process can just as easily be applied to the hundreds of tasks that people undertake every day as part of their ongoing roles and functions.

2. Motivation

   A good vision helps crystalise the benefits of a project by explaining why the extra effort that is required is worthwhile. Being able to demonstrate this pictorially is extremely motivating for most people, particularly those who think visually. As a result, a vision can help motivate people to take actions that start to move them in the right strategic direction.

3. Coordination

   A vision, a strategy and a technical plan also helps coordinate the actions of people and teams much more efficiently. Because having a vision and strategy simplifies the decision-making process, people can much more rapidly align their activities.

   This enables you, as a manager, to co-ordinate the actions of people in an extremely efficient manner. In addition, a vision, strategy, and plan are a good way to keep the coordination costs of a specific project to a minimum.

Putting a Vision and Strategy into Context

Once you have developed an appropriate vision and strategy, you will need to explain it to individual members of your team, in particular your line managers. By doing this, you can then work together to create a detailed implementation plan with specific steps and timetables.

Then you need to create a budget which reflects your overall strategy and implementation plan in terms of financial projections and specific costs.

Chapter 2

How do I Create a Vision and Strategy?

The process for creating a vision can be broken into four specific steps:

Step 1. First Draft :

> The process generally begins with an opening assertation from a single individual, reflecting real marketplace needs and their dreams

Step 2. Role of the Engagement Representatives

> This first draft will be modelled and then re-modelled over a few weeks by you and your Engagement Representatives, usually in a focus group setting. (See Appendix F for more details on focus groups). In establishing and managing these focus groups, you will need to consider the following four attributes:

> a. *Importance of Teamwork*

> > The focus group process never works well unless there is a high degree of effective teamwork.

> b. *Role of the Head and Heart*

> > In a focus group setting, everyone needs to have a mixture of analytical thinking and imagination throughout the process

> c. *Messiness of the Process*

> > Vision creation normally follows a route of two steps forward and one back, over a twisting, turning path. Do not expect it to be a simple, straightforward process.

> d. *Timeframe*

> > A vision is rarely completed in a single meeting. It may take months, even years. For this reason it is important that you maintain a sense of urgency, otherwise you may never find the time, finalise your vision or successfully implement your project.

Vision and Sport

The Australian Cricket Board (ACB)

The ACB's aim is to ensure the continued supremacy of Australian cricket by producing a steady flow of players of Test-match quality, creating the future by putting together a comprehensive development programme that begins in primary schools and finishes on the most famous cricket pitches around the world.

Williams F1 – We are all Racers Here

"What really makes Williams tick is that it is one huge great family and every single member of that family has got one vision. That is to be a winner, whether that is by their technical contribution or in some other way. Every single one of us is completely focussed on one thing."

Jane Gorard, Media Manager.

Leadership Style in Phase 2

Your Communication Style

- Sensitive

- Passionate

- Energetic

- Empathetic

Your Focus of Attention

- Displays an allegiance to all co-workers (above, below and beside them)

- Shows an understanding of how others are feeling

- Makes others feel valued and important

- Creates a workplace environment where colleagues feel they can try new approaches and take risks

- Looks for the unique contribution all colleagues can make to the team

- Encourages the team to be honest and open

Key Questions

- What is positive about the past

- Who or what do we need to confront in order to resolve this issue?

- Will this inspire our people?

- Does this solution help us deliver on our agreed 'one team' vision?

- To resolve this effectively, what constraints on our thinking or behaviour do we need to remove?

- How will we empower people to deliver on this solution?

Your Deliverables

- Passion

- Meaning

- Identity and symbols

- Authenticity

- Aesthetically pleasing environment

Chapter 2

How do I Create a Vision and Strategy? (cont)

Step 3.   Additional Drafts

Usually your Engagement Representatives together with other key players will work with you to re-draft your vision until it is complete.

Step 4.   The End Product

This process should result in a vision that has the following attributes:

a. *Imaginable*

Your vision should convey a picture of what the future will look like.

b. *Desirable*

Your vision should appeal to the long-term interests of employees and other stakeholders.

c. *Feasible*

Your vision should involve realistic and attainable goals. If your vision seems impossible to achieve it will be perceived as lacking credibility and thus fail to motivate your team and other people into action.

d. *Focused*

Your vision should be clear enough to provide guidance when it comes to decision-making.

e. *Flexible*

Your vision should be general enough to allow individual projects and alternative responses to reflect ever-changing conditions.

Strategy Development

In their study of 243 organisations, Turner and Crawford found that a significant part of a strategy must be to plan to develop resources to implement the vision.

Resources include :

- Systems and processes

- Personal

- Physical

- Technological

Turner and Crawford add these three hints when developing your resources and training your staff.

- Make sure you understand your future

- Include senior managers in the training

- Retrain from within

How do I Create a Vision and Strategy? (cont)

f. *Communicable*

Your vision should be easy to communicate and successfully explained in five minutes or less.

g. *Ambitious*

Your vision should be ambitious enough to force people out of their comfortable routines to achieve, to be the best at what they do, or have large percentage improvements.

Conversely a vision that requires only a slight improvement in performance or targets over a year will never force people to fundamentally re-think what is required of them in a rapidly changing environment.

h. *Increasingly Better Product at Lower Prices*

In a general way, your vision should aim to involve increasingly better products or services and lower costs, thus appealing to customers and shareholders alike.

i. *Trendy*

Your vision should take advantage of primary trends, especially new technology and globalisation.

j. *Ethical*

Your vision should not endeavour to exploit anyone and should thus have a certain moral power.

k. *Metaphoric*

Your vision should include a metaphor that matches your organisation's culture.

For example, part of a vision could be changed from "We need to retain our production rate yet improve our quality of product with after sales service in order to retain our existing customers and build additional sales in this competitive and tough environment."

to:

"We need to become less like Kia producers and more like a Mercedes production with after sales service."

How do I Create a Vision and Strategy? (cont)

Similarly if your employees love golf or sport, consider using a metaphor that includes golf or sport when describing your vision and strategy. Metaphors that work well tend to involve significant images in society such as Ferraris, cockroaches and mosquitos.

 I. *Symbolically Aligned*

 Make sure the symbols you use are properly aligned with your vision. More of this later.

Management Symbols – YOUR Actions Speak So Loud I Can't Hear What You're Saying

It has often been said that actions speak louder than words. This is also true when it comes to unveiling the vision for your project, in particular what you name your project, how you launch it and your ongoing style of communications.

Remember, different actions can mean different things to different groups of people. You need to ensure the symbols you use are relevant and convey the right messages to the people you are seeking to target.

For example, if your stakeholders are down-to-earth practical people with limited literacy then you will need to consider using images such as sporting or everyday metaphors.

If for example you were naming this project, instead of calling it 'A plan to increase levels of Education to IEEE standards' you may be better calling it 'A plan for building know-how'.

And when it comes to launching this project, instead of inviting everyone to a five-star restaurant and serving caviar, you may prefer to have a family day barbecue.

When it comes to ongoing communications to support this project, instead of using email-based surveys which assume that everyone is literate and has access to a PC, you may be better to use face-to-face and hard copy letters sent to people's homes.

Examples of Good Visions

Below are two examples of good visions.

Example A
Automated Mail Sorting System

It is the goal of the Automated Mail Sorting System (AMSS) to become a world leader in mail sorting within ten years. Here leadership means lower cost, faster delivery, faster processing and fewer errors.

These features will serve its interdepartmental and external client needs. It will make the workplace a more attractive place to work than any other in its field. Achieving this ambitious objective will surely require double digit cost reduction each year.

This vision has the following key attributes:

- It provides focus

- It states a clear target of being Number 1 in the industry in ten years

- It is ambitious enough

Example B
Government Engineering Division

"The vision driving our department's re-engineering effort is simple. We want to reduce our costs by at least 30 per cent and increase the speed with which we can respond to customers by at least 40 per cent.

These are stretch goals but we know, based on the pilot project in Austin, that they are achievable if we all work together.

When this is complete, in approximately three years, we will have leap-frogged our biggest competitors and achieved all the associated benefits: better satisfied customers, increased revenue growth, more job security and the enormous pride that comes from great accomplishments."

This vision includes many attributes of a good vision. For example:

- It is ambitious enough to force people out of comfortable routines

- It takes advantage of fundamental trends in new technology

Chapter 2

Developing Your Key Messages for Phase 2

The following table provides a guide for the development of the key messages and the approach you will need to adopt during this phase. This communication can take place with formal channels including presentation, noticeboards, newsletters, emails, telephone messages or informal channels such as informal face-to-face communication and hallway conversations.

LEVERAGE AREA	KEY MESSAGE TO BE COMMUNICATED
Feeling Valued and Respected	• Communicate the process for developing the new vision and strategy, and why it must be developed. • Involve the Engagement Representatives in your strategy development.
Gaining Recognition	• Acknowledge the role individuals and teams are playing in the development of the vision.
Making a Unique Contribution	• Develop an identity by creating an icon based on the simplest piece of equipment or role in the project.
Striving for Technical Excellence	• Start the vision sessions with a five minute trend analysis, statistical data and the organisation's wider strategy. • Integrate with your performance management system.
Understanding Political Motivation	• Communicate a compelling rationale for your strategy. • Encourage identification of weaknesses in your strategy. • Create opportunities for employees to ask questions and make sure you fully answer these questions .
Celebrating and Innovating	• When your strategy is complete, get senior management to launch the finished strategy to all those who will be key contributors. • Organise a number of senior managers to help celebrate completion of your vision and strategy.
Taking Practical Action	• Communicate the topline objectives. • Reinforce and communicate the key milestones and the tasks to be completed.
Being Listened To	• Seek feedback from Engagement Representatives for your vision and strategy.
Taking Personal Responsibility	• Communicate how your project is the responsible approach to solving an issue or problem.

Evaluating Phase 2

Best Guess Self-Assessment

You can use the following optional questionnaire to help evaluate the progress you and your team are making in successfully completing Phase 2. This questionnaire is designed to measure the effectiveness of your vision and strategy.

Just as for Phase 1, if you choose not to use the questionnaire you will need to complete all of the actions described in 'Actions to Create or Improve the Vision' and 'Actions to Create Practicality – Creating Strategies'.

To complete the questionnaire, please mark each question out of 10. A score of 0 means your answer strongly disagrees with the question, while a mark of 10 means your answer strongly agrees with the question.

If you neither agree nor disagree with the question because you believe it is not relevant to your situation or you do not know the answer to the question, then you need to give it a mark of 5.

Best Guess Survey

SECTION	Vision Desirability: with regard to this project	SCORE out of 10

QUESTION

1. Your project's vision and your explanation for why your recommended changes are necessary are compelling. ☐

2. Your managers understand and believe in your vision. ☐

3. Your Board and/or senior management team understand and believe in your vision. ☐

4. You can describe your vision within five minutes in a manner that ignites a reaction which signifies both understanding and interest. ☐

5. If your vision becomes a reality, it will have a positive impact on the organisation as a whole and its stakeolders in terms of meeting financial expectations. ☐

6. If your vision becomes a reality, it will have a positive impact on employees in terms of transforming them from frustrated workers to engaged employees by capturing their hearts and minds. ☐

7. Your vision identifies the heart of your stakeholders, your team or your organisation. ☐

Total Division Desirability Score ☐

Best Guess Survey (cont)

SECTION	Practicality (Quality of Strategies): with regard to this project	SCORE out of 10
	QUESTION	
	1. You have faith that your strategy will help you achieve your project objectives.	
	2. Your Engagement Representatives have faith in your strategy and it will help to achieve your vision.	
	3. Your managers understand and believe in your strategy.	
	4. The planned launch of your project symbolically matches your agreed vision well.	
	5. The name you have given to your project symbolically matches your agreed vision.	
	6. The communication style you plan to use supports your project, symbolically matching your agreed vision.	
	7. Your Board and/or Senior Management understand and believe in your strategy.	
	Total Practicality (Quality of Strategies) Score	

Interpreting the Results/The Resulting Actions

If you choose to complete the Self-Assessment questionnaire, you can now plot your scores on the Phase 2 Self-Assessment Chart following.

Plot your score from the Vision Desirability section on the X-axis and your score from the Practicality (Quality of Strategies) section on the Y-axis. This tells you what quadrant you are in. If you did not complete the Self-Assessment survey then assume you are in quadrant B. Then, using this quadrant letter, look up the table following to clarify your recommended action.

PHASE 2 Best Guess Diagnostic

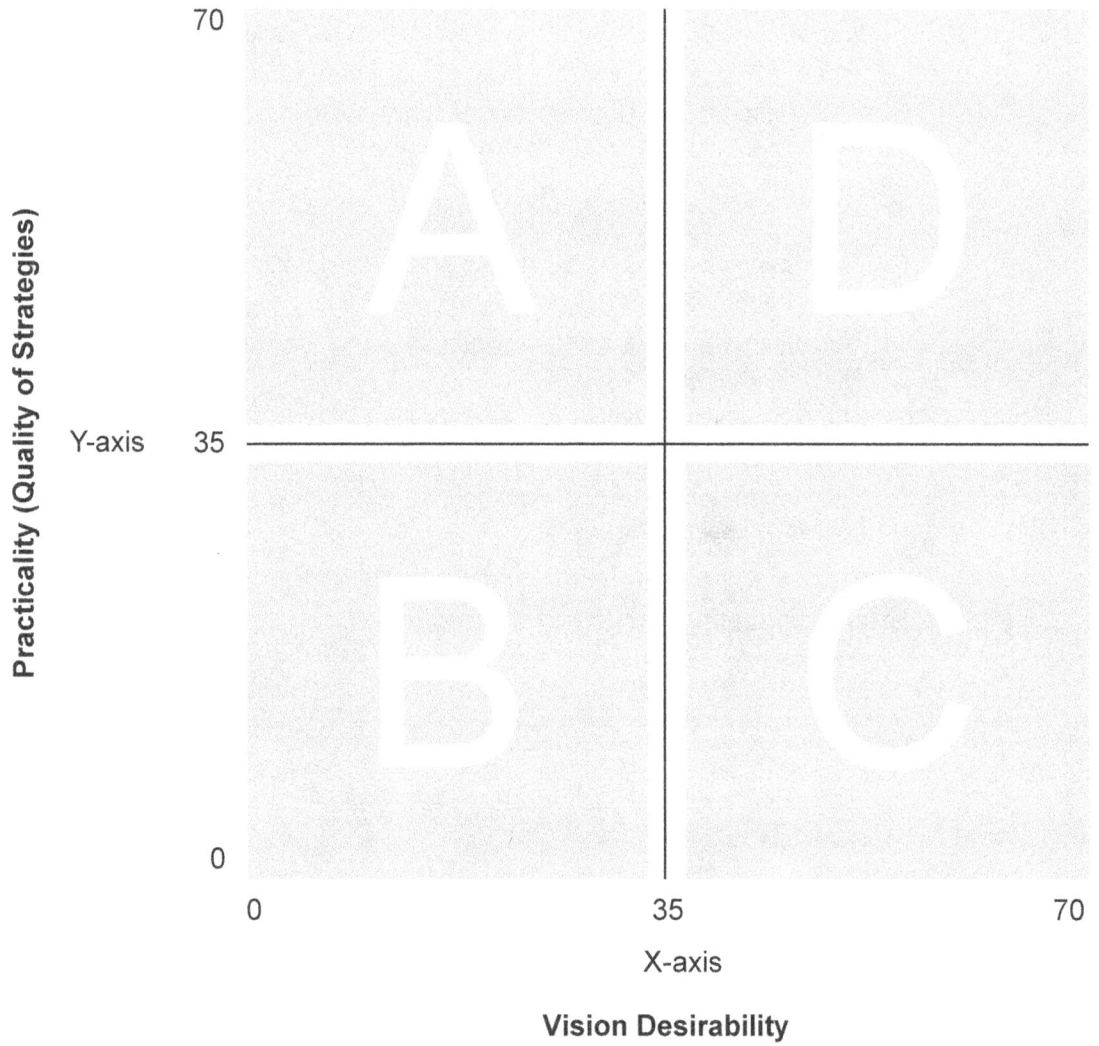

Practicality (Quality of Strategies)

Y-axis

70

35

0

0   35   70

X-axis

Vision Desirability

Interpreting the Results/The Resulting Actions

Quadrant	Diagnosis	Action Required
A	If you find yourself in quadrant A, you need to take further action to improve Vision Desirability.	**Improve your vision:** • Ensure your vision has the 12 key attributes of a good vision. To do this your vision will need to be: imaginable, desirable, feasible, focused, flexible, communicable, ambitious, increasingly better product at lower prices, trendy, ethical, metaphoric, and symbolically aligned. • Implement some or all of the actions in the section 'Actions to Improve Vision and Strategy - the Nine Motivators in the Overview Chapter'.
B	If you find yourself in quadrant B, you need to take further action to improve Vision Desirability and Practicality.	**Improve your vision and practicality:** • Ensure your vision has the 12 key attributes of a good vision. That is, imaginable, desirable, feasible, focused, flexible, communicable, ambitious, increasingly better product at lower prices, trendy, ethical, metaphoric and symbolically aligned. • Implement some or all of the actions in the section 'Actions to Improve Vision and Strategy - the Nine Motivators'. • Ensure your vision is feasible.
C	If you find yourself in quadrant C, you need to take further action to improve Practicality.	**Improve your practicality/strategies :** • Ensure your vision is feasible. To do this you may have to reduce how ambitious your vision is. In doing this, be careful you do not reduce it so far that you get to the point where the changes you are proposing are no longer perceived as being necessary. • Find the balance between being too ambitious. The ability to do this well is often the mark of a good leader. • Implement some or all of the actions in the section 'Actions to Improve Vision and Strategy - the Nine Motivators".
D	If you find yourself in quadrant D, you have successfully implemented this phase effectively.	You are ready to move to the next phase.

Repeat this self-assessment until you find yourself in quadrant D, at which point you can review the Phase 2 checklist to ensure all the necessary tasks have been completed. At this point you can move on to Phase 3.

Phase 2 Checklist

When you can tick each item in the following checklist, you are ready to move to Phase 3

☐ I have a vision and strategy created in conjunction with your Engagement Representative Team.

☐ My vision has the 12 attributes of a good vision: imaginable, desirable, feasible, focused, flexible, communicable, ambitious, increasingly better product at lower prices, trendy, ethical, metaphorical and symbolically aligned.

☐ I have selected a name for my project that is aligned with my vision and that my people can relate to.

☐ I have developed the key messages for this phase, based on the Nine Levers of Change.

☐ I have involved and informed the board and executive team of my project's vision and strategy, and the first draft of the launch approach.

Actions to Improve Vision and Strategy – the Nine Motivators

Your vision, strategy, and tactical plans also need to be grounded in terms of the nine motivators explained in the Overview.

To achieve this, select actions from three of the areas listed. Choose one item from each colour group. In doing this you will ensure that your actions will appeal to the widest range of people.

Chapter 3

PHASE 3: Communicate the Initiative and Engage the Team

Introduction

Having completed all of the required steps in Phase 2, you and your team are now ready to move onto Phase 3. The aim of Phase 3 is to create an increased sense of teamwork and, through effective communications, ensure all stakeholders not only understand but believe wholeheartedly in your project.

One of the key requirements of Phase 3 is to comprehensively communicate your project not just to your team but throughout the rest of the organisation. This is an enormous task but a vital one if you are to successfully build teamwork and improve overall morale.

A major part of your success in doing this will depend on how well you engage other people to communicate the details and benefits of your project on your behalf. To do this you will need to take action to ensure your vision and strategy appeals to the people you are hoping will implement it.

Key Topics Covered in this Chapter

In this Chapter you will explore:

- The importance of effective communication

- Benefits of engaging your team

- Effective communication strategies

Chapter 3

PHASE 1	PHASE 2	PHASE 3	PHASE 4	PHASE 5	PHASE 6
Instil Urgency, form Guiding Alliances and Set Clarity and Integrity	Develop Vision and Strategy	Engage the team and communicate the stratey.	Get broad-based actions and short-term wins	Consolidate gains and more change	Close with a celebration

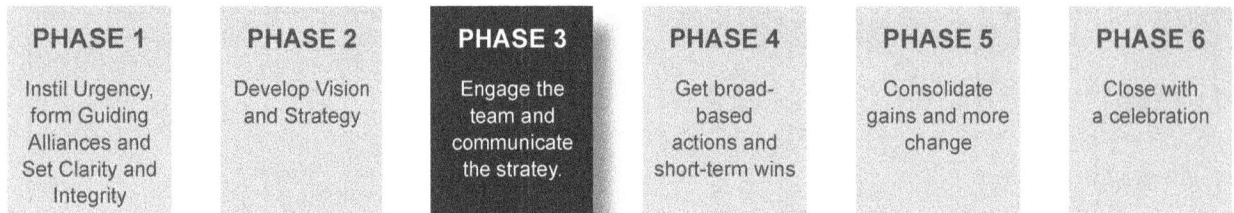

What does it mean to Engage and Communicate?

Phase 3 is very much about working together as a team towards a shared and common vision as well as specific, relevant, and realistic goals. To engage and communicate with your team you need to explain, visualise, and demonstrate your vision and goals in a simple, relevant, and credible manner.

Unless your team believes your vision and goals are achievable and can see a role for themselves in achieving these objectives, they are likely to become increasingly complacent, resistant to change and fragmented as a team. The simplest way to engage and communicate with your team is to ask yourself this question – how can I get everyone to work together to achieve our shared goals?

Why do You Need to Communicate by Engaging Your Team?

According to extensive studies by Crawford and Turner, the only way any project will succeed is by everyone working together as a team. At the start of the Engagement Process it is likely there will be competition with considerable internal fighting over limited resources, with one team cutting the other down to get ahead of the game.

If this is the case, before you can successfully implement your project you will need to change this environment to one of co-operation and teamwork. The only way you will do this is by engaging your team to effectively communicate your vision, strategy, and plan.

To demonstrate all of the above objectives, we will now take a look at a case study taken from the extensive studies of Crawford and Turner to see the consequences of failing to communicate.

Case Study:

The Consequences of Failing to Communicate

> *The CEO of an Australian engineering company has been asked to prepare a report on how a group of managers in the engineering division developed a vision and strategy for introducing a new approach to quality assurance.*

Why do You Need to Communicate by Engaging Your Team? (cont)

In seeking to implement and communicate their vision and strategy, this group of managers invested a significant amount of time, effort and money to share it with the broader organisation. This effort included undertaking a series of branch-level presentations, numerous articles for the organisation's newsletter and a variety of all-staff emails.

As part of his report and to measure the return on this investment, the CEO has surveyed a number of middle managers to see what level of support and understanding there is for the project's vision and strategy.

The results of this survey indicated that the majority of employees, including middle managers and senior executives, are in a state of complete denial about the existence of any such vision or strategy. What this means is that although important key messages had been disseminated, nobody had received or embraced them.

As part of this survey, many of the line managers, when pushed, admitted that they had heard 'something about clients and alignment but were not sure what it all meant.' The more candid managers said they thought it was all about 'jaw movement and that it obviously meant some pin head had been promoted who was going through the motions of justifying his own role and position.'

It would come as no surprise that the new approach was not adopted by the organisation.

The point of sharing this case study with you is that it demonstrates that when communicating the detail and benefits of your project, you need to remember that in most large organisations there is often a lot of information that has to be shared and processed each day.

According to research by Turner and Crawford, a typical employee will have to process around 4.3 million words every three months. To effectively communicate a vision and strategy will require around 20,000 words. This means that this vital information constitutes less than half of one per cent of an employee's total communications during a three-month period.

Chapter 3

What Does All this Mean?

The previous example clearly demonstrates that even if you successfully implement the first two phases of the Engagement Process perfectly, there is still a high risk that your initiative will fail if you have been unable to effectively communicate your vision, mainly due to the enormity of the task.

This is because getting hundreds or thousands of people to understand and support your vision, to the point where they are willing to change their behaviour, daily routine, and general approach, is a huge and challenging task.

The solution for overcoming this challenge is to engage people as a means of building a teamwork culture, one in which people are willing to share the task of communicating your vision and strategy.

What are the Benefits of Engaging the Team to Communicate Your Vision?

If you successfully engage your team to communicate your vision, you can look forward to vastly increased team morale, motivation, commitment, and ownership. But to achieve this level of engagement you will need to make sure you avoid the following pitfalls:

- **Telling people** - if you insist on instructing people or delivering 'let me tell you' speeches, you will be perceived as ignoring your employees' hopes, fears and expectations. This approach may work in the short-term but it will prove to be very hard work in the longer term.

- **Telling and selling** - if you continually try to persuade people without any opportunity for open discussions, even your most compelling reasons will not hold sway in the longer term.

- **Consulting** - if you continually seek to 'consult' people you risk being perceived as having made up your mind beforehand

To successfully engage your team you need to share the problem solving and decision-making processes with those who will be responsible for implementing the changes you are recommending.

By adopting this approach, you will begin to build commitment, support and ownership for your project. As a result, a willingness to adapt and compromise will begin to occur naturally.

Of particular value to you during Phase 3 is the ownership you create within your team. This will prove particularly vital as you begin to implement change.

Leadership Style in Phase 3

Your Communication Style

- Encouraging

- Sympathetic

- Persuasive using emotion and empathy

Your Focus of Attention

- Acknowledges and considers others opinions in a respectful and non-judgmental way

- Considers the opinions of others with an open mind

- Seeks out, listens to and considers the opposite viewpoint on any given subject

- Offers support to colleagues who may be experiencing difficulties

- Stands up for what they believe is right

- Stands by their actions without fear of reprisals or consequences

- Solves problems as they arise without fuss and drama

- Encourages the team to innovate or adapt if necessary to ensure a quality result

- Encourages other team members to be courageous in thought and deed

Key Questions

- Who needs to be involved and how will we negotiate with them?

- What would be a diplomatic approach to this situation?

- How can we build a real sense of teamwork?

- How genuinely does the proposed action reflect both our leadership team and the wider organisation?

- What control systems do we have in place to keep implementation on track?

- How can we make more courageous decisions?

- How can we use ingenuity to address some of the aspects of this problem?

- What does this solution enable us to do?

Your Deliverables

- People feel helped and supported

Chapter 3

What are the Benefits of Engaging the Team to Communicate Your Vision? (cont)

This is because ownership helps create:

- **Sufficient commitment** - to overcome people's natural resistance to change.

- **Sufficient desire** - to ensure your project succeeds by causing your team and other employees to become interested in doing what needs to be done.

- **Organisational-wide integration** - people from different parts of the organisation will become involved in building your project.

By engaging your team to communicate your project you will also create an environment where there is:

- **Less blame** - poor communications in support of a specific project are often blamed for people's general resistance to change as well as the limited intellect of some lower-level employees. The problem here is that this blame is being placed squarely on the shoulders of others rather than at the feet of the person seeking to communicate the vision and strategy. This approach works against team spirit because the very act of blaming others for the failure of the project actually adds to the reasons why it failed in the first place.

- **Strong team morale** - working with others to communicate a common cause builds strong team morale. This, in turn, prepares people to make more sacrifices as they become necessary in the process because they are focused on ensuring the shared vision is achieved.

- **A feeling of fun** - doing things as a team can be a lot more fun than doing things alone.

Communicate the Strategy

Woolworths the Fresh Food People

Turner and Crawford looked at Woolworths as an ideal case of *communicating the strategy*. After recording a $35m loss, Woolworths changed their approach to being 'The Fresh Food People'. When they introduced a new advertising campaign it was directed as much to their 35,000 employees as it was to potential customers.

The advertisements involved actual Woolworths staff showing interest, confidence, commitment and excitement. The advertisements were everywhere, on brochures, cars, store walls, internal documents and radio. The focus on the Woolworths' people was also important. The critical fact was that it was impossible to work for Woolworths and not be aware of its vision and where its future would lie.

What is the Process for Engaging Your Team to Communica the Your Vision?

The process for engaging your team to communicate your vision involves using your 'Engagement Representative' team in a focus group setting. (See Appendix F for more details on managing Focus Groups). This will enable you and your 'Engagement Representatives' to plan how your vision can be shared throughout the organisation and seek to ensure everyone is working towards a shared vision.

Some Effective Communications Strategies

John P Kotter found the following steps vital for effective communications:

- **Trial Run** - test out your proposed communications on your 'Engagement Representatives' by asking them to respond in a way that the other employees are likely to. If they react negatively then you can be sure that your proposed approach will generate an even more negative reaction to your communications when they are unveiled to a wider audience.

- **Sell the Benefits** - when communicating your vision you need to clearly explain the benefits of this vision, particularly at a personal level and not just at an organisational level. To do this you need to use simple, relevant language that explains why the changes you are seeking to make are attractive for all employees. You will also need to provide employees with some reassurance about the changes you are proposing becoming a reality.

- **Use Multiple Forms of Communications** - when seeking to implement effective communications you need to use every possible vehicle to explain your vision and strategy. This will mean sending out as many memos or newsletters as possible, each explaining the changes you are proposing, the progress you are making, the short-term wins you and your team are achieving, and the long-term impact of your initiative.

  You will also need to use both verbal and written communication as well as tools such as posters, email, large and small team/employee meetings as well as other types of formal and informal interaction.

  You will also need prepared memos, presentations and briefing packs to ensure you and your team are delivering consistent key messages and can easily leverage every opportunity that comes your way to deliver your key messages. You will also need to ensure that your own actions and those of the Board reflect the changes and vision you are trying to achieve.

Chapter 3

Some Effective Communications Strategies (cont)

- **Repetition** - the key messages you use about the detail and benefits of your initiative will only be absorbed if they are repeated time and time again. In general, most people will measure the importance of the information they are given based on the number of times it is repeated to them.

- **It is also important to use the Nine Motivators** - different people learn and absorb information in different ways. To ensure that everyone hears your key messages, you will need to communicate them using the following methods. By doing this you will ensure that your key messages appeal to the widest range of people.

Developing Your Key Messages for Phase 3

The following table provides a guide for the development of the key messages and the approach you will need to adopt during this phase. This communication can take place with formal channels including presentation, noticeboards, newsletters, emails, telephone messages, or informal channels such as informal face-to-face communication and hallway conversations.

AREA	KEY MESSAGE TO BE COMMUNICATED
Feeling Valued and Respected	• Create open communication where team members get to know and respect how to best work with each other.
Gaining Recognition	• Train the key managers and other change leaders on how to present, acknowledge, reward, and recognise those teams contributing to the project.
Making a Unique Contribution	• Emphasise the unique contribution each team member is making.
Striving for Technical Excellence	• Involve the technical employees in workshops where they share their insights on the particular processes, tools, or equipment you're introducing.
Understanding Political Motivation	• Explain the political wisdom of teamwork and create a forum for asking questions.
	• Create opportunities for employees to ask questions about this particular Phase and then ensure you answer them fully.
Celebrating and Innovating	• Encourage the formation of cross-functional teams to solve problems.
Taking Practical Action	• Encourage an environment of total commitment.
Being Listened To	• Communicate the feedback you receive across the organisation as a whole.
Taking Personal Responsibility	• Insist on a team orientation rather than an individual approach. Link this with the values of the project and the values of the organisation.

Chapter 3

Evaluating Phase 3

Best Guess Self-Assessment

You can use the following optional questionnaire to help evaluate the progress you and your team are making in successfully completing Phase 3. This questionnaire is designed to measure how well you have communicated the project and engaged the team. Just as in Phase 1 and Phase 2, if you choose not to use this questionnaire you will need to complete all the actions in 'Improving Communicating the Vision' and 'Improving Engaging the Team'.

To complete the questionnaire, please mark each question out of 10. A score of 0 means you disagree strongly with the question while a mark of 10 means you strongly agree with the question.

If you neither agree nor disagree with the question because you believe it is not relevant to your situation or you do not know the answer to the question, please give the question a mark of 5.

Best Guess Survey

SECTION	Communicating the Vision: with regard to this project	SCORE out of 10
	QUESTION	
	1. Most of your stakeholders know what your vision is.	
	2. The average stakeholder can describe your vision.	
	3. Most of your stakeholders believe in the benefits your project will deliver.	
	4. Most of your stakeholders believe the project is a good thing overall.	
	5. You have repeated the message of the vision.	
	6. You have used different forums to communicate the vision.	
	7. Most of your stakeholders believe in the consequences of *not* implementing your project.	
	Total Communicating the Vision Score	

Chapter 3

Best Guess Survey (cont)

SECTION	Engaging the Team: with regard to this project	SCORE out of 10
	QUESTION	

1. The average stakeholder communicated your vision to other stakeholders. ☐

2. Different divisions communicated your project to other divisions. ☐

3. You have consulted with your team to communicate the vision and strategy. ☐

4. Morale has increased as a result of spreading the vision as a team. ☐

5. People feel supported as they spread the vision. ☐

6. Emotional needs are being met as stakeholders spread the vision. ☐

7. Goodwill has spread amongst stakeholders as they spread the vision. ☐

Total Engaging the Team Score ☐

Interpreting the Results/The Resulting Actions

If you completed the Self-Assessment survey you can now plot your scores on the Phase 3 Self-Assessment Chart following. Plot your score from the Communicating the Vision section on the X-axis and the score from Engaging the Team on the Y-axis.

This tells you what quadrant you are in. If you did not complete the Self-Assessment survey then assume you are in quadrant B. Then, using this quadrant letter, look up the table following to clarify your recommended action.

PHASE 3 Best Guess Diagnostic

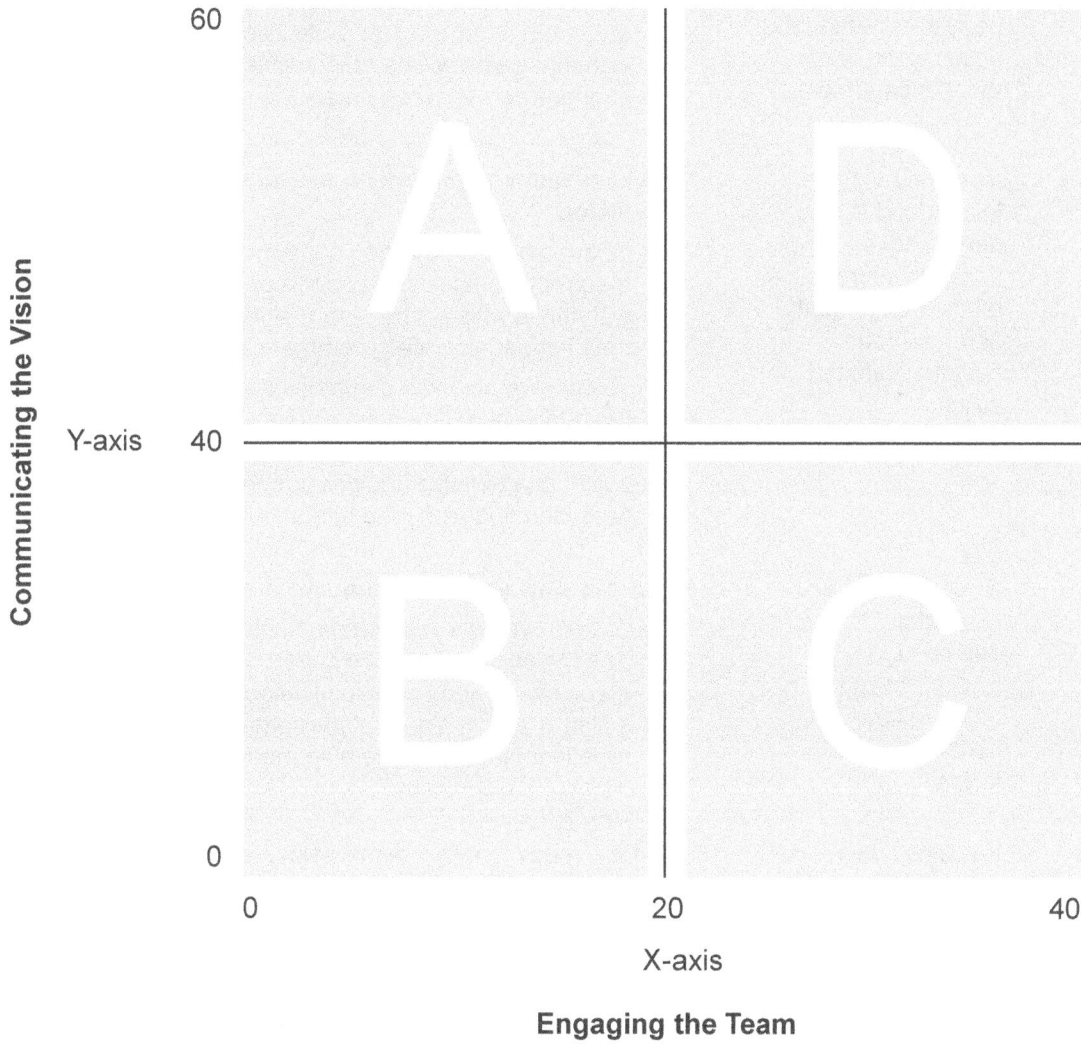

Interpreting the Results/The Resulting Actions

Quadrant	Diagnosis	Action Required
A	If you find yourself in quadrant A, you need to take further action to improve team engagement.	**Improve team engagement:** • To successfully engage your team you need to share the problem-solving and decision-making processes with those who will be responsible for implementing the changes you are recommending.
B	If you find yourself in quadrant B, you need to take further action to improve team engagement and how you communicate the vision.	**Improve team engagement and how you communicate the vision:** • To successfully engage your team you need to share the problem- solving and decision-making processes with those who will be responsible for implementing the changes you are recommending. • To improve how you communicate your vision you need to ensure you have covered all of the key elements of 'good communications' including trial runs, selling the benefits, multiple communications forums, repetition and using the nine motivators.
C	If you find yourself in quadrant C, you need to take further action to improve how you communicate the vision.	**Improve how you communicate the vision:** • To improve how you communicate your vision you need to ensure you have covered all of the key elements of 'good communications' including trial runs, selling the benefits, multiple communications forums, repetition and using the nine motivators.
D	If you find yourself in quadrant D, you have successfully implemented this phase effectively.	You are ready to move to the next phase.

Repeat this self-assessment until your scores place you in D quadrant, at which point you can review the Phase 3 checklist to ensure you have taken all the necessary tasks to complete Phase 3. Once you have done this you are then ready to move onto Phase 4.

Phase 3 Checklist

When you can tick each item in the following checklist, you are ready to move to Phase 4.

☐ I have used the Engagement Representatives to get the organisation working as a team with a shared vision and strategy.

☐ I have built strong teamwork and overall morale as part of this process.

☐ Most stakeholders know what the project is, the benefits it will deliver, and what its overall impact will be.

Chapter 3

Chapter 4

PHASE 4: Get Broad-Based Action and Short-Term Wins

Introduction

Having completed the required activities in Phase 3 you and your team are now ready to move on to Phase 4.

Now that you have got your people working well as a team, towards a shared vision using strengthened relationships, you are ready to empower your people, break through the glass ceiling of performance and achieve short-term goals.

This is the main focus of Phase 4 which is all about breaking down barriers and working as a committed team to achieve short term wins as you drive forward the implementation of your project. These barriers may include the way the organisation or particular divisions or teams are structured, people or teams having the wrong or incomplete skills set, the organisation's human resources systems not being aligned to the agreed vision and supervisors or managers who go out of their way to continually block change.

The key to overcoming these barriers is to empower people to implement your project by encouraging them to take risks, make changes and develop creative ideas at work. To drive the implementation of your project you will need to achieve short-term wins but these will need to be systematically planned, created and then advertised widely within the organisation.

Key Topics Covered in this Chapter

In this Chapter you will explore:

- Achieving broad-based action

- Empowering your people

- Getting some short-term wins

Chapter 4

PHASE 1	PHASE 2	PHASE 3	PHASE 4	PHASE 5	PHASE 6
Instil Urgency, form Guiding Alliances and Set Clarity and Integrity	Develop Vision and Strategy	Engage the team and communicate the stratey.	Get broad-based actions and short-term wins	Consolidate gains and more change	Close with a celebration

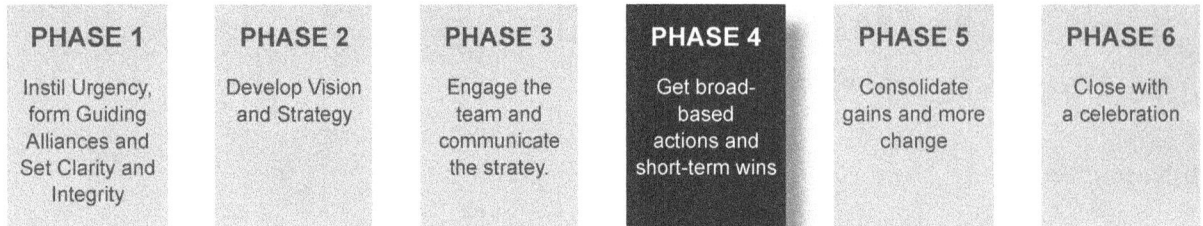

All Talk and No Work

Up until now, your focus has been on talking, planning and communicating but there has not been a lot of 'doing'. This all changes in Phase 4 as you begin to look at breaking through barriers and begin to implement your objectives by empowering others to take broad-based action and set as well as achieve short-term goals.

What is Broad-Based Action?

Broad-based actions are activities that are implemented across the organisation. It is where stakeholders act as a team to start implementing your project.

What Does Empowering People Mean?

Empowering people means helping them become more powerful and enabling them to use their strengths as a team. To do this you must break down barriers that are interfering with, or preventing you from implementing your project and achieving short-term wins.

Leadership Style in Phase 4

Your Communication Style

- Decisive
- Courageous
- Persistence
- Fair
- Intense
- Magnanimous
- Energising

Your Focus of Attention

- Ensures all team members 'walk the talk'
- Aligns the activity of the group with the vision of the organisation
- Ensures systems are practical and understood by the people using them
- Considers the wider organisational impact of key decisions or changes made in their area
- Puts forward suggestions to improve work practices and work flows
- Encourages the team to take a strategic approach and focus on undertaking right action

Key Questions

- Is this team looking at this issue independently and without political interference?
- What is the real underlying issue that we need to address?
- Do we have the capability we need to address this, or do we need to bring in someone from outside the group?
- Are we getting too fragmented in our discussion, rather than looking at the big picture issue?
- What strategic framework are we using to address this issue?

Your Deliverables

- Resolution of conflict
- Any decisions that were unresolved get resolved
- A feeling of drive and passion in the team

Chapter 4

What are the Key Barriers to Empowering People for Broad-Based Action?*

There are four key barriers to empowerment, all of which need to be broken down if your project is to succeed. These barriers are:

1. Structures

To successfully implement your project it is likely you will need the help of different divisions or sections. These people will need to work together, something that can be extremely difficult and frustrating unless you create proper cross-functional teams.

For example, if your project requires you to improve customer focus but the organisation's structure is such that responsibility for delivery of products and services is fragmented, you will need to break down this structural barrier if you are to succeed.

You will do this by giving more responsibility to lower-level employees and ensuring that their broad-based actions are not blocked by layers of middle-managers who may criticise and undermine your short-term actions as well as your project as a whole.

2. Skills

You will need to make sure that people have the right skill-set to implement your project. Attitude training may also be necessary to empower others in a team context.

3. Human Resources System Alignment

Your formal human resources systems will need to be aligned with the agreed vision and your overall project. This includes the organisation's formal people management tools such as performance evaluation, recruitment and promotions processes and systems.

4. Blocking Supervisors

Nothing discourages people more than obstructive and difficult supervisors or managers. People who discourage broad-based actions as part of implementing your project, must be confronted.

*Taken from John P Kotter *Leading Change*

How Do You Empower People?

As well as removing the barriers to implementing your project, people can also become empowered through encouragement of risk-taking. If people are to embrace your project, some risks will have to be taken. That is they will have to start doing things that previously were not appreciated or accepted as 'what we do'. If you are to empower people to implement your project you will need to encourage them to take risks.

These risks include asking them to throw out their old rulebooks and making changes, not just to how they do things but also encouraging other people to change how they do things. All of this will require ingenuity and creativity. That is why it is vital for you and your team to encourage non-traditional ideas, activities, actions and all other forms of ingenuity and creativity.

What is a 'Win'?

A win is any visible improvement that is linked to your project.

What are Short-Term Wins?

Short-term wins are about reaching interim goals that partly deliver the key objectives of your project. For example, if your project is to increase productivity by 100 per cent over 10 years, a short-term win would be achieving a 15 per cent increase in productivity after 18 months.

Manage the Action – Drive the Wins

In their study of 243 organisations, Turner and Crawford found four key options for getting things done to achieve the intended outcomes. They are:

1. Direct involvement. Sometimes direct involvement from senior management works best to push staff towards following a project.

2. Intensive use of resources, strong implementation and enforced trading policies.

3. Align senior management activities and environments with the project.

4. Perform regular performance reviews, aligning performance with the project.

Chapter 4

Short-Term Wins

What are the Benefits?

According to John P Kotter's extensive research, short-term wins provide six key benefits:

1. **Evidence it was worth the sacrifice** - wins help justify the short-term costs or sacrifices that are usually associated with change.

2. **Encourage change agents** after putting in a significant amount of hard work, positive feedback helps build morale and motivation.

3. **Fine-tune vision** - short-term wins give your 'Engagement Representatives' tangible data to show the feasibility of their ideas.

4. **Undermine cynics** - unmistakable performance increases make it difficult for people to oppose change.

5. **Keep bosses on side** - wins provide more senior people in the hierarchy with proof that the Employee Engagement process is on track.

6. **Build momentum** - wins can turn neutrals into supporters, reluctant supporters into active helpers, and active helpers into helpers that are more resilient to attack.

How Do You Achieve Short-Term Wins?

John P Kotter's research found the following five tasks are critical to achieving short-term wins:

1. Focus on the strengths

2. One-in, all-in; All or nothing attitude

3. Lead from the front

4. Advertise your wins – you can do this by visibly recognising and rewarding people who have helped make wins possible. Once you start achieving short-term wins it is important you spread the word about what is being achieved. This will give you a chance to provide examples of achievable and valuable goals. To be a short-term win something must be:

   Visible - any number of people must be able to see the result for themselves and this result needs to be real and not just hype

   Clear - there must be no room for people to argue about the attributes or detail of the short-term win

   Linked to the project - it must be obvious that the result is part of your project

   The first short-term win target - once you have achieved one short-term win make sure people are focused on the next win and so on

5. Be systematic - you must make a systematic effort to guarantee unambiguous wins within 6 to 18 weeks. Actively look for ways to deliver clear performance improvements by establishing goals as part of the quarterly planning system. When an objective is achieved, reward the people involved with recognition, promotion or some kind of financial reward.

Developing Your Key Messages for Phase 4

The following table provides a guide for the development of the key messages and the approach you will need to adopt during this phase. This communication can take place with formal channels including presentation, noticeboards, newsletters, emails, telephone messages, or informal channels such as informal face-to-face communication and hallway conversations.

AREA	KEY MESSAGE TO BE COMMUNICATED
Feeling Valued and Respected	• Communicate to all team leaders how everyone is going, to encourage teamwork and train mentors.
Gaining Recognition	• Reward success publicly – use tools such as a monthly CEO email.
Making a Unique Contribution	• Emphasise the reasons for achieving specific goals and the importance of your project to the organisation as a whole. • Recognise passionate responses to living the corporate promise.
Striving for Technical Excellence	• Encourage specialists to identify how the organisation can maximise the changes that are being made.
Understanding Political Motivation	• Explain why changes are happening, why some areas are performing better than others. • Create opportunities for employees to ask questions about progress to date and make sure you answer these questions fully.
Celebrating and Innovating	• Celebrate key milestones achieved by teams. • Encourage innovation and new approaches.
Taking Practical Action	• Focus on strengths. • Foster a 'will do' attitude. • Tell stories of practical 'right' actions. • Encourage an attitude that does not tolerate a lack of commitment to achieving corporate goals.
Being Listened To	• Encourage suggestions, comments, and improvements from employees about how the project is affecting them.
Taking Personal Responsibility	• Create clear objectives. • Make it clear what the rewards are for compliance and the consequences of non-compliance. • Promote responsible goal-centred behaviour.

Chapter 4

Evaluating Phase 4

Best Guess Self-Assessment

You can use the following optional questionnaire to help evaluate the progress you and your team are making in successfully completing Phase 4.

This questionnaire is designed to help measure how effectively you are breaking down barriers and empowering people. Just as in Phases 1, 2 and 3, if you choose not to use the questionnaire you will need to complete all the actions in 'Improving Broad-Based Actions' and 'Improving Short-Term Wins'.

To complete the questionnaire give each question a mark out of 10. A score of 0 means you disagree strongly with the question while a mark of 10 means you agree strongly with the question. If you neither agree nor disagree with the question because you believe it is not relevant to your situation or you do not know the answer to the question then please give the question a mark of 5.

Best Guess Survey

SECTION	**Communicating the Vision: with regard to this project**	**SCORE out of 10**

QUESTION

1. You have no major structural obstacles blocking your project such as inter-divisional barriers.

2. People have the correct and complete skill sets and attitudes for your project.

3. You have aligned your human resources systems with your project.

4. Supervisors are not working against or blocking your project.

5. With regard to this project, you have no other blockages in areas.

6. You put things in place so you won't have blockages to your project in the future.

7. Implementation of your project is broad-based or organisation-wide.

Total Broad-Based Action Score

Chapter 4

Best Guess Survey

SECTION	Communicating the Vision: with regard to this project	SCORE out of 10
	QUESTION	
	1. You have no major structural obstacles blocking your project such as inter-divisional barriers.	☐
	2. People have the correct and complete skill sets and attitudes for your project.	☐
	3. You have aligned your human resources systems with your project.	☐
	4. Supervisors are not working against or blocking your project.	☐
	5. With regard to this project, you have no other blockages in areas.	☐
	6. You put things in place so you won't have blockages to your project in the future.	☐
	7. Implementation of your project is broad-based or organisation-wide.	☐
	Total Short-term Wins Score	☐

Interpreting the Results/Actions to be Undertaken for Phase 4

If you chose to complete the Self-Assessment questionnaire, you can now plot your scores on the Phase 4 Self-Assessment Chart following. Plot your score from the Short-Term Wins section on the X-axis and your score from the Broad-Based Action section on the Y-axis.

This tells you what quadrant you are in. If you did not complete the Self-Assessment survey then assume you are in quadrant B. Then, using this quadrant letter, look up the table following to clarify your recommended action.

PHASE 4 Best Guess Diagnostic

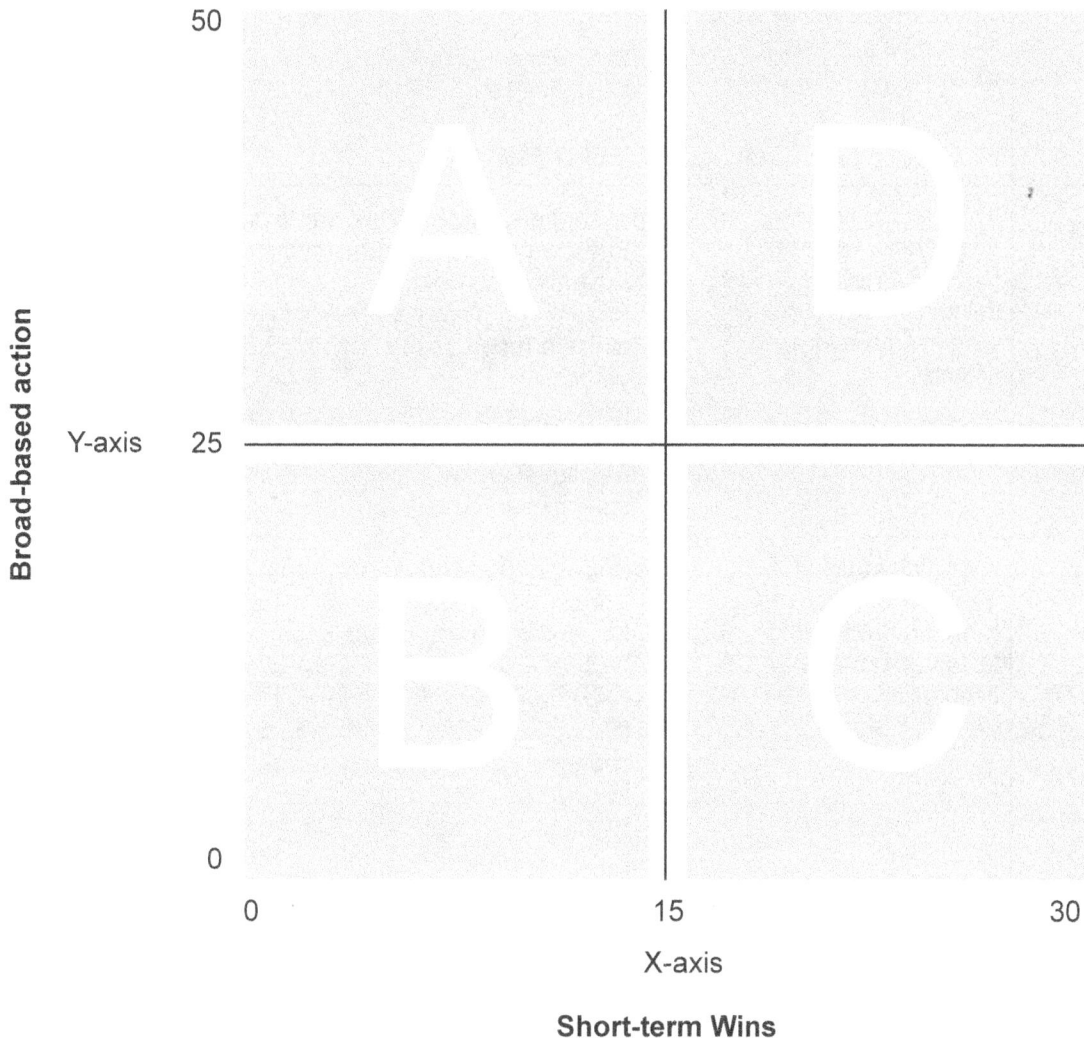

Interpreting the Results/The Resulting Actions

Quadrant	Diagnosis	Action Required
A	If you find yourself in quadrant A, you need to take further action to improve short-term wins.	**Improving Short-Term Wins:** Follow this five-point plan to achieve short-term wins: 1. Plan 2. Create wins 3. Advertise your wins 4. Set short-term win targets 5. Be systematic
B	If you find yourself in quadrant B, you need to take further action to improve short-term wins and broad-based action.	**Improving short-term wins and broad-based action:** • Set short-term win targets and create wins • Advertise your wins • Ensure you have no barriers to empowering people to achieve broad-based action. (Refer page 69 for more details) • Encourage risk-taking • Encourage people to develop and implement non-traditional ideas, activities, actions and other forms of ingenuity and creativity
C	If you find yourself in quadrant C, you need to take further action to improve broad-based action.	**Improving Broad-Based Action:** • Ensure you have no barriers to empowering people to achieve broad-based action. These barriers may include structural barriers, the wrong or incomplete skill set, non-alignment of human resources systems with the agreed vision, or supervisors/managers who block change • Encourage risk-taking • Encourage people to develop and implement non-traditional ideas, activities, actions and other forms of ingenuity and creativity
D	If you find yourself in quadrant D, you have successfully implemented this phase effectively.	You are ready to move to the next phase.

Repeat this self-assessment until your scores put you in D quadrant, at which point you will be ready to review the Phase 4 checklist to ensure you have completed all of the required tasks before you move on to Phase 5.

The Nine Motivators

Your action items for getting broad-based action and short-term wins also need to be grounded in terms of the nine motivators explained in the Overview

Select actions from three of the areas listed in the 'Developing Your Key Messages' table on page 65. Choose one item from each colour group.

In doing this you will ensure that your actions appeal to the widest range of people.

Phase 4 Checklist

When you can tick each item in the following checklist, you are ready to move to Phase 5.

☐ There are no major barriers obstructing implementation of the project. (Potential barriers include structural barriers, the wrong or incomplete skills set, human resources systems not being aligned to the agreed vision and supervisors/managers who block change).

☐ I have created an environment that encourages risk-taking and creativity.

☐ To get short-terms wins I have systematically created a plan, created those wins and advertised the wins.

Chapter 5

PHASE 5: Analyse the Gains and Produce More Change

Introduction

Having completed the required activity in Phase 4 you and your team are now ready to move on to Phase 5.

The focus of Phase 5 is on analysing what you have done during the past four phases and then building further momentum by improving on these achievements. In doing this you will need to look closely at what has worked well and what went poorly.

To do this you need to undertake research so you can build insight and near-perfect knowledge about your project and the changes you are implementing. Done well, this analysis will provide you with clarity about what activities you should cut out of your implementation plan, those that you should keep, how you can capitalise on your strengths and if you should adjust or refine your overall goals based on what you know now and have achieved to date.

As a result of this analysis, you will also identify further changes you need to introduce based on your new-found insight. These changes may include the introduction of new processes and tools, updating of overall goals, removal of any excess resources, and avoidance of battles that you and your team are unlikely to win.

Overall, the key to successfully completing Phase 5 is the quality of the analysis you undertake which will form the basis of the opportunities you create in Phase 6.

Key Topics Covered in this Chapter

In this Chapter you will explore:

- Analysing what is and is not working

- Creating a system to duplicate high performance

- Refining your implementation plan with lessons learnt

Chapter 5

PHASE 1	PHASE 2	PHASE 3	PHASE 4	PHASE 5	PHASE 6
Instil Urgency, form Guiding Alliances and Set Clarity and Integrity	Develop Vision and Strategy	Engage the team and communicate the stratey.	Get broad-based actions and short-term wins	Consolidate gains and more change	Close with a celebration

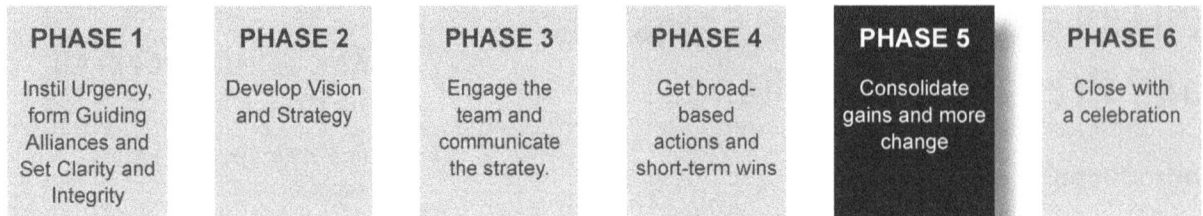

Why Do We Need Analysis and More Change?

By now, having reached Phase 5, you and your team will have seen your agreed vision increasingly becoming a reality as you continue to achieve key milestones and short-term wins.

Given the progress you are making, it would be easy to fall into the trap of celebrating your achievements and letting things continue at the same rate of progress without pushing even harder to drive through your project. The danger in doing this is that inevitably your rate of progress will begin to slow and then to fall.

This is because, as most of us know from first-hand experience, organisations do not embrace change quickly. To achieve even the smallest amount of change, many employees often have to work over and above the call of duty. It is therefore natural that they should want to take a bit of a breather, even though this will slow things down and could be disastrous for the specific project and organisation as a whole.

During his extensive research into organisational change, John P Kotter found that if there is a sense that the pressure is now off and the focus shifts to celebrating what has been achieved to date, organisations rapidly lose momentum and can backslide, undoing all the changes and improvements that had been achieved. On top of this, he also found that once this happens, organisations find it even harder to then try and re-ignite the change process.

John P Kotter's research showed that organisations which successfully implemented major change were those that, at this stage in the process, focused their efforts on:

- Constantly analysing their achievements to ensure any excesses are removed even if this includes making people redundant

- Introducing even more change

- Maintaining a sense of urgency

He also found that when this analysis is done well, organisations are able to build smart tools and processes that can be used to significantly streamline projects and improve the rate at which change is achieved.

Leadership Style in Phase 5

Leadership Style in Phase 5

- Your Communication Style
- Respectful
- Keeps confidences
- Calmness in crises

Your Focus of Attention

- Stands up for what they know is right
- Displays supportive/protective behaviour for their colleagues
- Creates a sense of security/stability within the team
- Effectively plans work with clear milestones and systems of reporting
- Identifies and manages the risks associated with completing individual or team objectives
- Encourages colleagues to develop their technical knowledge and skills
- Creates clear audit trails related to activity or key decisions
- Learns from mistakes and documents this learning so that other team members can benefit
- Shows respect for colleagues' knowledge/expertise
- Rationally considers the facts before making key decisions
- Encourages others to show team members respect

Key Questions

- Are we taking the right amount of responsibility for the right things?
- How can we take the role that this group is playing and move it to a higher level of performance?
- Have we made this decision based on our shared principles?
- How can we be disciplined in our decision-making?
- Are we being objective?
- What specialist knowledge or analysis can we incorporate into our decision-making?
- From a systems mastery approach, what impact will our decision have?
- Have we leveraged from all the internal expertise available?

Your Deliverables

- Detailed plans
- Complete understanding of all relevant facts, processes and implications of the initiative
- A refined and powerful strategy

Chapter 5

Why Do We Need Analysis and More Change? (cont)

This analysis also provides clarity around what activities should continue as part of the change implementation plan and those that should be cut. It also helps identify areas where significant savings can be achieved.

What Analysis Do You Need to Do?

In analysing your progress to date, your aim is to gain insight and understanding about your project and everything it interacts with. The reason for this is that it will enable you to see:

- The progress you are making

- What actions and activities delivered positive results and why

- What actions and activities worked poorly and why

- How people felt at each part of the process and how they reacted to specific actions and activities

- What the risks are

- How close to completion you are

- The current market environment

- Whether your goals are still relevant or need fine tuning, and

- What further information people need to be able to complete your project and achieve the agreed vision

Depending on your specific organisation and the project you are trying to implement, this analysis phase may require you to produce a series of reports such as a gap analysis, an environmental scan and analysis, an employee survey and a market environment report.

If your project involves increasing client satisfaction and demand, then some of the outcomes of Phase 5 will need to focus on various client satisfaction and market surveys. If your project is focused on increasing productivity you will also need to include an employee productivity survey.

Analysis Outcomes

The outcomes of your analysis are primarily about finding and reusing processes that have worked well and building new, more relevant and appropriate processes and tools for the areas that have not worked so well.

If you have successfully created an environment of increased risk-taking and creativity in the previous phases, there will be a myriad of 'good' processes that employees are now comfortable with and that are also well documented.

That said, in order to keep driving through your project and ensure your rate of progress does not slip, you will still have to build even more tools and processes to continually clarify what steps and actions worked and which ones did not.

Developing your Key Messages for Phase 5

The following table provides a guide for the development of the key messages and the approach you will need to adopt during this phase. This communication can take place with formal channels including presentation, noticeboards, newsletters, emails, telephone messages, or informal channels such as informal face-to-face communication and hallway conversations.

AREA	KEY MESSAGE TO BE COMMUNICATED
Feeling Valued and Respected	• Increase the profile of individuals that are working smarter not harder.
Gaining Recognition	• Recognise technical excellence, clever processes, strategies and achievement of team goals.
Making a Unique Contribution	• Focus on the ways in which the organisation is achieving its purpose and raising standards. • Focus on people who are making a special or unique contribution.
Striving for Technical Excellence	• Communicate how you are identifying high performance teams and are duplicating their approach across the organisation. • Communicate your progress using a series of analysis models and tools.
Understanding Political Motivation	• Explain why more change is needed. • Identify potential performance problems . • Create opportunities for employees to ask questions about this phase and ensure you answer these questions fully.
Celebrating and Innovating	• Encourage creative approaches and cross functional input.
Taking Practical Action	• Communicate the teams strengths and solidarity. • Encourage a culture that feels the pain but carries on with change anyway for the benefit of everyone.
Being Listened To	• Encourage feedback on how you can keep the change process and momentum on track.
Taking Personal Responsibility	• Encourage updating of systems and processes to ensure best practice across the organisation.

Evaluation Phase 5

Best Guess Self-Assessment

You can use the following optional questionnaire to help evaluate the progress you and your team are making in completing Phase 5. This questionnaire is designed to measure the effectiveness of your analysis and the degree of clarity you have created about your implementation plan.

Just as in previous phases, if you choose not to use the questionnaire you will need to complete all the actions in 'Improving Your Analysis' and 'Creating More Change'.

To complete the questionnaire, give each question a mark out of 10. A score of 0 means you disagree strongly with the question while a mark of 10 means you agree strongly with the question.

If you neither agree nor disagree with the question because you believe it is not relevant to your situation or you do not know the answer to the question please give it a mark of 5.

Best Guess Survey

SECTION	Analysis of Gains: you have perfect knowledge about	SCORE out of 10

QUESTION

1. Your project regarding the progress you are making and how close you are to completion. ☐

2. All the things that interact with your project including external parties and the overall morale of employees. ☐

3. Future risks regarding the project. ☐

4. Your project's actions that worked well. ☐

5. Your project's actions that worked poorly. ☐

6. The current market environment relating to the project. ☐

7. How people felt at each part of the process of introducing the project and how they reacted to specific actions and activities. ☐

Total Analysis of Gains Score ☐

Best Guess Survey

SECTION	Creating More Change: you have	SCORE out of 10
	QUESTION	

1. Comprehensively identified all the processes employees can use now to implement your project.

2. Comprehensively developed new tools and processes that replace poorly performing processes that employees can use to implement your project.

3. Confidence that your visions and goals as well as your overall project are still valid in your market environment and today's world.

4. Perfect knowledge about what further information people need to be able to complete your project and achieve the agreed vision.

5. Clarified what actions in your implementation plan should be removed as they did not work well.

6. Implemented any significant savings.

7. Ensured any excesses are removed.

Total Creating More Change Score

Interpreting the Results/Actions to be Undertaken in Phase 5

If you chose to complete the Self-Assessment questionnaire, you can now plot your scores on the Phase 5 Self-Assessment Chart following.

Plot your score from the More Change section on the Y-axis and your score from the Analysis section on the X-axis. This tells you what quadrant you are in. If you did not complete the Self-Assessment survey then assume you are in quadrant B. Then, using this quadrant letter, look up the table following to clarify your recommended action.

Chapter 5

PHASE 5 Best Guess Diagnostic

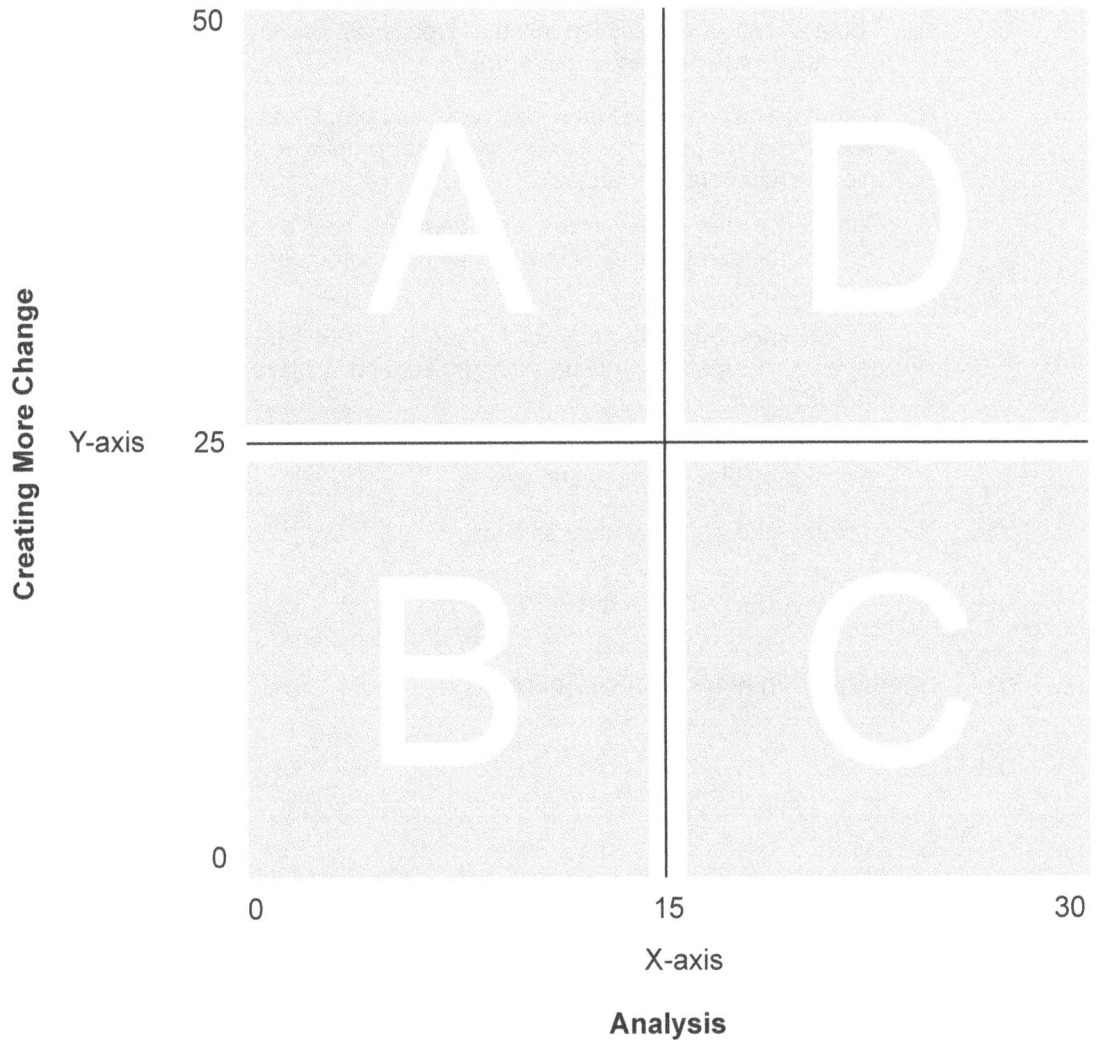

Interpreting the Results/The Resulting Actions

Quadrant	Diagnosis	Action Required
A	If you find yourself in quadrant A, you need to take further action to improve your Analysis.	**Improving analysis:** • Depending on your project, you may need to prepare a number of reports including: • A review of your market environment • A review and analysis of your stakeholders • A gap analysis that clearly identifies the gap between where you are currently and what you are trying to achieve with your project in the long-term
B	If you find yourself in quadrant B, you need to take further action to improve your Analysis and Create More Change.	**Improving your analysis and creating more change:** • Prepare more reports such as a review of your market environment, a review and analysis of your stakeholders and a gap analysis. • Use your analytical data to simplify your process models and review other projects using your newfound clarity. You need to do this because routine tasks often involve more steps and people than is necessary. At the same time, it will also become obvious that some of your other planned projects are no longer critical to your initiative or are doomed to fail.
C	If you find yourself in quadrant C, you need to take further action to Create More Change.	**Creating More Change:** • Use your analytical data to simplify your process models and review other projects using your newfound clarity. You need to do this because routine tasks often involve more steps and people than is necessary. At the same time, it will also become obvious that some of your other planned projects are no longer critical to your initiative or are doomed to fail.
D	If you find yourself in quadrant D, you have successfully implemented this phase effectively.	**You are ready to move to the next phase.**

Repeat this self-assessment until you find yourself in D quadrant, at which point you need to review the Phase 5 checklist to ensure all the necessary tasks have been completed. You and your team can then move on to Phase 6.

Chapter 5

The Nine Motivators

Your action items for achieving effective analysis and even more change need to be grounded in terms of the nine motivators explained in the Overview.

Select actions from three of the areas listed the the developing your key messages table on page 86. Choose one item from each colour group. In doing this you will ensure your actions appeal to the widest range of people.

Phase 5 Checklist

When you can tick each item in the following checklist, you are ready to move to Phase 6

☐ I've done enough research and analysis to have near perfect knowledge about my project.

☐ I have found or created a number of process models that improve the speed and efficiency of how things are done.

☐ I have removed any unnecessary activities within the organisation

Chapter 5

Chapter 6

PHASE 6: Anchor the Initiative in the Culture

Introduction

Having completed all of the required steps in Phase 5, you and your team are now ready to move onto the final part of the Employee Engagement process. The focus of Phase 6 is on cementing and 'anchoring' your project in the organisation's culture through the use of celebrations and leveraging of your newly formed relationships. (The organisation's 'culture' simply means the way we do things around here). This final part of the engagement process is all about forming new alliances and focussing on the future.

Of specific importance to the success of Phase 6 is your understanding that 'anchoring' is very much a communications activity that can only be appropriately applied at the end of the process. It is also vital for you to understand and appreciate that anchoring involves not only positive but also sometimes negative activities such as making people redundant. To successfully implement these initiatives, they have to be fully aligned to your project.

Overall, Phase 6 is a fun and high-energy period that requires extensive creativity and a willingness to solve old problems in new ways. To implement this phase well you will need to encourage people to celebrate and let go of their 'old ways' to fully embrace new processes and tools.

You will do this by using the positive mood you have created during the previous phases to cement your initiative into the present culture. You will also successfully anchor your initiative by reminding people about the negatives of the old culture.

Last but not least, Phase 6 provides a fantastic opportunity for you and your team to build new relationships and continue improving the organisation's processes and systems.

Key Topics Covered in this Chapter

In this Chapter you will explore:

- Anchoring the changes for good

- Looking to the future

Chapter 6

PHASE 1	PHASE 2	PHASE 3	PHASE 4	PHASE 5	PHASE 6
Instil Urgency, form Guiding Alliances and Set Clarity and Integrity	Develop Vision and Strategy	Engage the team and communicate the stratey.	Get broad-based actions and short-term wins	Consolidate gains and more change	Close with a celebration

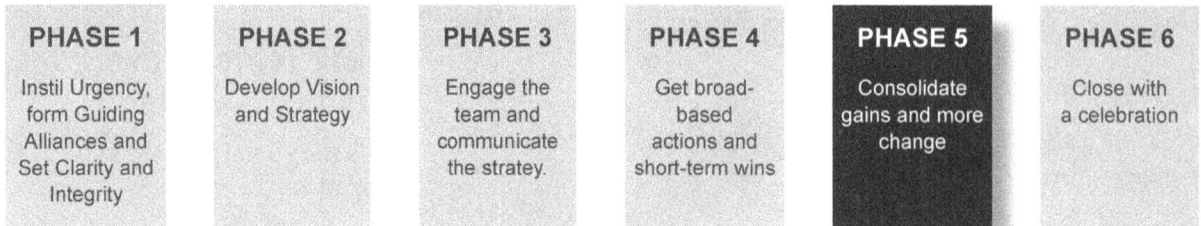

Why Do We Still Need to Spend More Time Anchoring the Project?

Without implementing Phase 6, you run the risk of everything you have achieved and all the positive changes you have implemented unravelling over time or when a major event occurs such as the CEO retiring or some of your 'Engagement Representatives' being re-located.

It is only by spending time celebrating your achievements and focusing on the positive changes that have been implemented that you will be able to guarantee that the time and effort you and your team have invested in the previous phases has been worth it.

This is because old, long-established cultures can take a very long time to die for three key reasons:

- Individuals are selected and taught the old ways so well

- An organisation's culture has many lives – in a large organisation culture exerts itself through the actions of hundreds or even thousands of people. This means that trying to isolate and change culture through small groups will often fail as people will tend to revert to their old ways as soon as they return to their familiar environments and teams

- Because organisational culture happens without much conscious intent it is difficult to discuss - let alone challenge

Leadership Style in Phase 6

Your Communication Style

- Tell stories

- Upbeat, high energy

- Imaginative

- Light

- Charming and disarming

- Playful

Your Focus of Attention

- Looks outside the organisation for innovative ideas that can be applied internally

- Seeks out challenging opportunities to test their skills and abilities

- Manages their time effectively so that they get done all things for which they are responsible

- Celebrates with a sense of satisfaction when a project is completed or a key milestone is reached

- Meets daily challenges with enthusiasm and energy

- Uses questions to clarify team member points of view, team objectives and procedures

Key Questions

- Increase the enthusiasm in this team around this issue?

- Where will we need to focus our drive in order to be successful?

- How can we turn around this disaster into something in our favour?

- Are we being entrepreneurial enough and taking advantage of the opportunities this presents?

- How can we use this situation to motivate the wider organisation?

Your Deliverables

- Considered many options

- Develop new relationships and alliances

- Created a fun environment for the team

How Do You Anchor Your Initiative in the Organisation's Culture?

To overcome the problems highlighted above, John P Kotter, in his research found that change in an organisation can only survive and remain anchored if the following five key rules are applied:

1. **Anchoring comes last** - anchoring a project must be left until the last stage of the process otherwise people in the organisation will not have seen enough positive results to internalise it and perceive the changes as being part of 'the way we do things around here'.

2. **Anchoring is results-dependent and results need to be shared** – here are a few examples of positive anchoring statements that you can use:

    *   'These results are typical of the previous culture but times have now changed'

    *   'These bad results occurred just before the project was introduced'

    *   'These results are about now and demonstrate that the project is now a part of us all.'

    *   'These results obviously show that our project was worth it because life is happier and easier for every individual and the organisation as a whole'

Anchoring statements need to be positive, shared enthusiastically and must associate the initiative with easier and more positive times. This is because one of the basics of psychology is that people tend to move towards positive reinforcement and away from negative reinforcement.

3. **Anchoring is a communications activity** - that is why Phase 6 is all about celebrating the 'death' of the old ways and being thankful for the new ways. This a key message that must be communicated at every opportunity - as part of CEO speeches to large groups through to small talk at after-work Friday night drinks.

4. **Anchoring may also involve negative actions** - organisations that successfully embrace and anchor projects require people to make difficult decisions such as seeing that some people take early retirement packages because they are struggling to embrace the 'new way of doing things'.

    Often these hard decisions can help remove the main antagonists to change and pave the way for you and your team to form new, stronger relationships with people who strongly support your project.

5. **Anchoring means making HR systems and other 'relationship building' tools dependent on the project** - this is particularly important when it comes to ensuring the changes can survive through major 'people' changes such as the appointment of a new CEO or Board members.

How Do You Anchor Your Initiative in the Organisation's Culture? (cont)

Ensuring these tools are aligned with your project will also be vital when it comes to acquiring new vendors and suppliers or the establishment of joint ventures and alliances as well as the recruitment of new employees.

New Relationship Opportunities

The process of anchoring through the integration of new, aligned relationships is a significant part of Phase 6. This is because the research you and your team undertook in Phase 5 will have clarified the many new opportunities you have to form relationships with other stakeholders who can help your cause. For example:

New employees may need to be recruited to implement some of the recommendations from previous phases.

It may be possible to simplify some process by using different and more integrated suppliers.

Economies of scale may be gained by forming alliances with other business partners.

In each of these examples, a new relationship will need to be formed, which is why it is critical that these new relationships epitomise your project.

Developing Your Key Messages for Phase 6

The following table provides a guide for the development of the key messages and the approach you will need to adopt during this phase. This communication can take place with formal channels including presentation, noticeboards, newsletters, emails, telephone messages, or informal channels such as informal face-to-face communication and hallway conversations.

AREA	KEY MESSAGE TO BE COMMUNICATED
Feeling Valued and Respected	• Communicate the lessons that have been learnt, the goals that have been achieved and new possibilities for the future.
Gaining Recognition	• Publicly reward high performing teams. • Create a Hall of Fame to support, recognise and encourage excellence.
Making a Unique Contribution	• Celebrate the purpose of the organisation and its achievements with external stakeholders. • Consider ways of discussing what is missing within the organisation - as you move forward.
Striving for Technical Excellence	• Set new benchmarks of performance.
Understanding Political Motivation	• Look at the challenges ahead and the changing political environment in which the organisation operates. • Create opportunities for employees to ask questions about this phase and ensure you answer these fully and in a timely manner.
Celebrating and Innovating	• Celebrate the changes that have been delivered with presentations similar to those used to originally launch your initiative.
Taking Practical Action	• Report successes to all key stakeholders. • Make new alliances with key stakeholders. • Encourage enthusiasm for celebrating the achievement of worthwhile goals.
Being Listened To	• Seek feedback about the process from internal and external stakeholders.
Taking Personal Responsibility	• Rewrite procedures and policies to bring them in line with the new improvements. • Standardise new approaches.

Evaluating Phase 6

Best Guess Self-Assessment

You can use the following optional questionnaire to help evaluate the progress you and your team are making in completing Phase 6. This questionnaire is designed to measure how effectively you have anchored your project in the organisation's culture and are building new relationships.

Just as in the other Phases, if you choose not to use the questionnaire you will need to complete all the actions in 'Improving Your Anchoring' and 'Improving Your Relationship Building'.

To complete the questionnaire, give each question a mark out of 10. A score of 0 means you disagree strongly with the question while a mark of 10 means you agree strongly with the question.

If you neither agree nor disagree with the question because you believe it is not relevant to your situation or you do not know the answer to the question please give it a mark of 5.

Best Guess Survey

SECTION   **Anchoring**   **SCORE out of 10**

QUESTION

1. With regard to this project, the change has become 'the way we do things around here.'

2. New recruits with leadership skills could easily be change leaders for this project.

3. You have communicated the positive results of the project.

4. With regard to this project, you have communicated the message that it is "death to the past" and we are thankful for the new.

5. Your HR systems and other relationship building tools are dependent on the project.

6. With regard to this project, there has been investigation into making negative decisions to embrace the project, such as seeing that some people go into early retirement if they are struggling to embrace the 'new way of doing things'.

7. There is a lack of antagonists confronting the project.

Total Anchoring Score

Best Guess Survey (cont)

SECTION	Relationship Building	SCORE out of 10

QUESTION

1. The new external relationships you are creating as a result of your achievements from the previous phases are aligned with your project.

2. The new employees that have been recruited recently are aligned with your project.

3. You held events such as BBQ's or family days to celebrate the success of your project and simultaneously build relationships for the project's future.

4. You have searched for new opportunities created by the project.

5. New relationships been formed to take advantage of realised opportunities relating to the project?

6. Relationships are being formed to position the organisation well in the future to benefit from growing opportunities related to the proejct.

7. Relationships are being formed to further support the project.

Total Relationship Building Score

Interpreting the Results/Actions to be Undertaken in Phase 6

If you chose to complete the Self-Assessment questionnaire, you can now plot your scores on the Phase 6 Self-Assessment Chart following. Plot your score from the Relationship Building section on the X-axis and your score from the Anchoring section on the Y-axis.

This tells you what quadrant you are in. If you did not complete the Self-Assessment survey then assume you are in quadrant B. Then, using this quadrant letter, look up the table following to clarify your recommended action.

PHASE 6 Best Guess Diagnostic

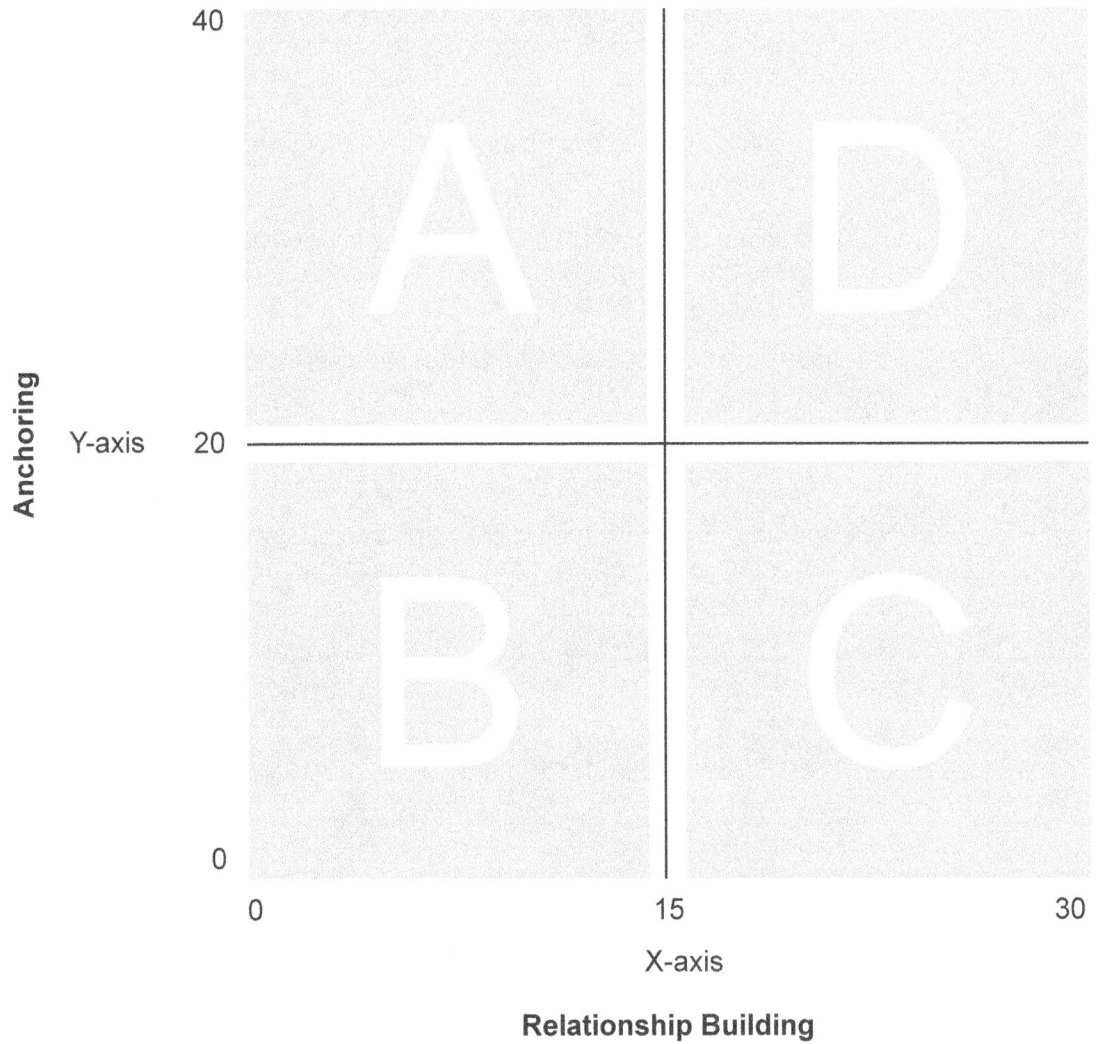

Anchoring

Y-axis 40 / 20 / 0

A | D
B | C

X-axis

0 15 30

Relationship Building

Interpreting the Results/The Resulting Actions

Quadrant	Diagnosis	Action Required
A	If you find yourself in quadrant A, you need to take further action to improve your relationship building.	**To Improve Relationship Building:** • Revisit the research you undertook in Phase 5 to clarify potential constructive relationships or alignments that need to be formed • Ensure all internal recruitment and communications processes are fully aligned with your project for both existing and new employees
B	If you find yourself in quadrant B, you need to take further action to improve your relationship building and anchoring.	**To Improve Relationship Building and Anchoring:** • Revisit the research you undertook in Phase 5 to clarify potential constructive relationships or alignments that need to be formed • Ensure all internal recruitment and communications processes are fully aligned with your project for both existing and new employees • Reiterate how the old culture was good for the past but no longer works in today's society • Discuss how the new culture helps solve issues and makes life easier as well as more enjoyable for everyone • Use examples that are based on the actual results your project has delivered • Be prepared to make the hard decisions such as seeing that some people retire early or making people redundant who are unable to embrace change
C	If you find yourself in quadrant C, you need to take further action to improve your anchoring.	**To Improve Anchoring:** • To improve your ability to anchor your project, John P Kotter, based on his extensive research into organisational change, recommends that you: • Reiterate how the old culture was good for the past but no longer works in today's society • Discuss how the new culture helps solve issues, makes life easier and more enjoyable • Use examples that are based on the actual results your project has delivered • Be prepared to make the hard decisions such as forcing people to retire early or making people redundant who are unable to embrace change • Ensure all new relationships are fully aligned with your project
D	If you find yourself in quadrant D, you have successfully implemented all phases effectively.	**No action. Phases are complete**

Repeat this self-assessment until you find yourself in D quadrant, at which point you need to review the Phase 6 checklist to ensure all the necessary tasks have been completed. You and your team will then have finished implementing the 6-phase Employee Engagement Process. Congratulations.

The Nine Motivators

The actions you take to anchor your initiative and build new relationships also need to be grounded in terms of the nine motivators explained in the Overview.

Select actions from three of the areas listed in the developing your key messages table on page101. Choose one item from each colour group. In doing this you will ensure that your actions appeal to the widest range of people.

Phase 6 Checklist

When you can tick each item in the following checklist, you are ready.

☐ I have applied the five key rules of anchoring.

☐ I have applied the relationship building opportunities defined in Phase 5.

Chapter 6

Chapter 7

Frequently Asked Questions

Throughout the Chapters in this handbook and the Appendices to follow, we have shared a great deal of information with you. As you begin to absorb this information and put it into action as part of your everyday roles, no doubt you will have questions about what we have shared with you and the 'Employee Engagement' process in general.

In this Chapter we have sought to anticipate the type of questions you may have and provide simple, easy to understand and grounded answers that will

help you better understand the 'Employee Engagement' process and the important role you have to play as a manager within your organisation.

General Questions

Q. **Why do we need a Handbook such as this? Does this mean that the organisation is going to be restructured again?**

A. This Handbook is designed to provide managers of all backgrounds and experience with an easy to follow process for effectively managing change, irrespective of the specific area you work in or the size of your team. Based on years of academic and practical research, it seeks to explain how new projects and change in general can be introduced into large organisations in a way that ensures maximum employee engagement as well as delivery the of tangible, measurable results within an acceptable timeframe.

Q. **In today's society, everyone faces constant change, both at work and in our personal lives. The way we respond to and manage change impacts not only our happiness but also our careers and long-term prosperity. Change in any organisation is often very difficult. As human beings we do not respond well to change and, as a result, sometimes we can react negatively and even aggressively to anything that we perceive as threatening our status quo.**

As a manager, you have a responsibility not only to your colleagues but also the general public to manage change effectively. In addition, as a manager you are part of a team committed to achieving best practice in everything done.

As a manager, you will have encountered considerable change over the past few years. These changes have developed and evolved the organisation into the organisation it is today but there is still more work to be done. As many managers will know from first hand experience, irrespective of your role or the projects you have sought to introduce, implementing change in any organisation can be extremely difficult.

This Handbook is part of your organisations commitment to you to provide you with the

Frequently Asked Questions (cont)

training and tools you need to be an effective, successful manager. It is also designed to provide you with a simple, standardised process for introducing change in a simple, action-based and results-focused way.

Q. Why is so much of the content based on the work of John P Kotter and of Turner and Crawford? Why is their research relevant to managers within my organisation?

A. John P Kotter is one of the most respected writers and researchers into organisational change. Based at the Harvard Business School in the US, John P Kotter has, over 30 years, undertaken extensive research into change management. He has written six best-selling business books together with two video/CD-ROM programs on the topic including his most successful book, Leading Change.

In preparing this Handbook, we have also drawn specifically from two Australian authors, Dennis Turner and Michael Crawford, who have conducted similar research across a total of 243 Australian organisations. In their book - Change Power – Turner and Crawford explain that change management is all about effectively managing your employees by ensuring they are engaged, empowered and influenced to succeed in an environment of change.

Dennis Turner is a Professor of Management at the Australian Graduate School of Management within the University of New South Wales. He has teaching and research experience as well as a commercial background in Chief Executive and other senior management roles in both the private and public sectors in Australia and the UK. Dr Michael Crawford is principal of a management consulting firm specialising in implementing change for Australian organisations. In this role he has, for many years, successfully combined his academic achievements with his extensive experience in systems analysis and management.

Q. What sort of projects can the 'Employee Engagement' process be used for?

A. As a manager, you will have encountered considerable change over the past few years. These changes have developed and evolved the organisation into what it is today but there is still more work to be done. As many managers know from first hand experience, irrespective of your role or the projects you have sought to introduce, implementing change in any organisation can be extremely difficult.

The 'Employee Engagement' process can be used for projects of all shapes and sizes. It is designed to provide you with a simple, standardized process that will help keep you and your teams on track as you continue to evolve and improve the specific area in which you work. It is equally applicable to large, medium and small projects or indeed any kind of change that you may need to implement.

Frequently Asked Questions (cont)

Q. **Is it compulsory for managers to use this process or do we have a choice?**

A. This Handbook is part of your organisations commitment to you, to provide you with the training and tools you need to be an effective, successful manager. It is also designed to provide a standardised process for introducing change in a simple, action-based and results-focused way. It is up to you to what degree you embrace and apply the process but the aim is to ensure that it becomes the standard approach for managing change and implementing projects.

The Employee Engagement Process
Phase 1

Q. **Why do you assume that people will be complacent, resistant or negative about change?**

A. Based on our own previous experiences of introducing change as well as the extensive research of change management specialists such as John P Kotter and Turner and Crawford, it has now been firmly established that many people, when faced with change, are either complacent towards, resistant to or negative about anything that is perceived as threatening the status quo.

Q. **Why is it so important to create urgency if a particular project is to be spread over, say, 18 months?**

A. Urgency is the key to overcoming people's complacency or resistance to change. It is important to create a sense of urgency as it will be much harder to ignite this sense of urgency in people if they have been allowed to ignore it from the outset.

Q. **How do you explain the benefits of your project in circumstances where there are going to be job losses and other changes that will not necessarily be beneficial in the short-term for some members of your team?**

A. This is part of the challenge of being a leader. Benefits come in many different forms. For those who lose the leadership of an old team but are gaining the leadership of a new one then the personal benefits are seen in the additional training and career growth they may attain. For those losing their jobs, there may be nothing you can do but ride out until their last day. In all cases the benefits to the team, the organisation, and the community should be highlighted.

Q. **What do you do if the consequences of not introducing your project are not particularly powerful or daunting in the short term and are therefore not likely to bother people that much?**

Frequently Asked Questions (cont)

A.   It is your task to make them powerful. If the benefits are not significant enough then look for legal or social implications. If this does not help then you may need to introduce further environmental inducements such as threatening that the department will need to be closed without the change.

Q.   **What do you do if you do not have the budget to reward your team as part of your project? Are there any other alternatives?**

A.   There are many rewards beyond just those that cost money. These include:

   •   Appreciation. A simple thank you and a smile means a lot to most people.

   •   Knowledge of benefiting the community. Knowing that innocent outsiders rely on you can be very motivational.

   •   Privileges. Having a car space or placard can be motivational.

   •   Task Choice. People often jump at the opportunity to be involved in things such as newer technology or more expensive machines.

   •   Career alignment. Everyone values doing work in line with their personal career goals. So point out the ways in which their tasks are in line with these career goals.

Q.   **What do you do if you are a new manager and you don't yet have the right employee connections but have been asked to introduce a major project or changes as part of your new role? How do you create a Guiding Alliance in these circumstances?**

A.   What you will know is who to ask, even if that is your supervisor. If you ask a few people who to ask and you get common names then you are probably on the right track.

Q.   **Does it matter what role or level your Engagement Representatives are? Do they have to be fellow managers or can you use all kinds of employees?**

A.   Your Engagement Representatives can be chosen from anywhere so long as they have the listed characteristics and there are key line managers among them. With this said, in looking for characteristics such as leadership, you would expect to turn to managers to see this.

Q.   **What if you do not yet have all the answers to create the required clarity you talk about in Chapter 1? What if you don't yet have clear job descriptions, cannot yet be clear about what is expected of people or what resources you are likely to need?**

Frequently Asked Questions (cont)

A. In these circumstances make sure you are clear enough to be able to implement the next stage.

Q. **Why are the organisation's corporate values a key part of creating integrity when it's clear currently very few people in the organisation actually understand or embrace them?**

A. If you believe that the values are not well known or embraced by your team then a key part of your role will be to educate people about them and encourage them to implement these values as part of your initiative. Without common goals or shared values, it can be extremely difficult to introduce change. The time you spend educating people about these values will stand you in good stead for ensuring the future success of your particular project.

Phase 2

Q. **Surely the vision we have should be one that is shared across the whole of the organisation? How can I have a vision for a particular project? Is a vision the same as an outcome or goal?**

A. The word vision is used in many contexts. In the context of the 'Employee Engagement' process, a vision is simply the big picture or a metaphor of what the future will look like when your project has been successfully introduced. The outcomes and goals of your project are all part of your vision and should be included in the very brief commentary about why the organisation should strive to build its future.

Q. **Do I need to get my vision, and indeed the process, signed off by the senior management team?**

A. In implementing your project, you will need to follow the normal sign-off procedures that apply to your everyday role.

Phase 3

Q. **How do I communicate my project to my team and throughout the organisation? Do I have to do the communicating myself or do I use the organisation's communications team or other suitable resources? How do I know whether I have the authority to do this?**

A. The resources you use and how you communicate the key messages about your project will depend on the exact circumstances. At a team level you should use your normal communications methods such as team briefings and one-on-one discussions with colleagues. If you require further help to communicate your initiative throughout the organisation, you should speak to your senior manager and/or discuss the other options that are available.

Chapter 7

Frequently Asked Questions (cont)

Q. **What do I do if I am not confident at speaking to bigger groups or am relatively new to the organisation and do not yet have the credibility or experience to engage people or encourage them to follow me?**

A. The best way to communicate with people and present yourself as a credible, inspirational leader are detailed in Chapter 2 of the Handbook. The key elements of effective communications include:

- Having a trial run with your Engagement Representatives

- Constantly selling the benefits of your project

- Using multiple communications forums

- Continually repeating your key messages

Q. **What do you do if you are struggling to get people to work as a team? Do you just move onto Phase 4?**

A. You cannot move onto the next phase until your scores on the self-assessment chart put you in D quadrant and you are able to tick all the items on the checklist as having been completed. If you do move on before you are ready, you risk undoing all the good work you have achieved to this point and your project ultimately failing to achieve the desired changes you are seeking to introduce.

Phase 4

Q. **How do I, as a manager, influence the organisation's HR systems? Surely this is outside of my role? How would I go about making sure they are aligned to my project?**

A. If you are not the HR Manager then you will not be able to merely tell the HR systems what to do. You will have to discuss and negotiate issues with mutual respect and listening. If you share the vision, the motivation of both the HR Manager and you will be strong and the outcome aligned.

Frequently Asked Questions (cont)

Phase 5

Q. **What is the point of spending time analysing what we've achieved to date. Why shouldn't I just keep ploughing on with the project? Won't I risk losing the sense of urgency and momentum I've created?**

A. The aim of analysing your progress to date is to gain insight and understanding about your project and everything it interacts with. The reason for this is that this research will enable you to see:

- The progress you are making

- What actions and activities have delivered positive results and those that have not

- How people felt at each part of the process

- How people have reacted to specific actions or activities

- What the continuing risks are

- How close you are to completing your project

- The current market environment

- Whether your goals are still relevant or need fine tuning

- What further information people need to ensure you can complete your project

All of this information will help ensure you and your team remains on track and are able to successfully take your project through to completion.

Q. **What do I do if the analysis shows that things are not going as well as I had thought and that my goals are not relevant anymore?**

A. If the research shows that your progress is not as strong as you had expected, you will need to revisit the action lists in Phase 5 to help improve your current position in the process. If necessary, you may want to revisit each Phase to ensure you completed all the necessary actions and did not move on too quickly.

Q. **Is it a bad thing if you find your goals are not relevant and need fine-tuning? What does this mean to the process and our overall project?**

A. No it is not a bad thing if you have to refine your goals as this is all part of the process. It will also ensure that your project is continuing to evolve and remains aligned with the organisation as well as current market conditions.

Frequently Asked Questions (cont)

Phase 6

Q. **What sort of celebrations are suitable for inclusion in Phase 6, and who should pay for them? Should we mainly do team-specific things or get everyone involved within the organisation?**

A. How you choose to celebrate your achievements to date will depend on the exact circumstances. At a team level you should use your normal methods such as after-work drinks, maybe a team BBQ or family day. If you require further help or want to seek additional funding to celebrate the results you've achieved you should speak to your senior manager and/or discuss the other options that are available.

Q. **How do I go about sharing the results of what we've achieved with everyone in the organisation? Do I do that myself or get help from say the organisations' communications team?**

A. The resources you use and how you communicate the results you have achieved will depend on the exact circumstances. At a team level you should use your normal communications methods such as team briefings and one-on-one discussions with colleagues. If you require further help to communicate the results throughout the organisation, you should speak to your senior manager and/or discuss the other options that are available.

Appendix 1

The Art and Science of Transformational Leadership

Transformation is a word often used to describe the emotional aspect of organisational change. While the word is bandied about by management consultants and authors alike, very rarely do leaders get it right. In this article Peter Burow explores the history, science and art of transformational leadership and the link between ancient insight and some of the latest findings from neuroscience and organisational change.

Your Employees are the Result of Millions of Years of Perfection

Charles Darwin proposed a radical theory - that human beings, over the past two to three million years, have evolved through a process of 'survival of the fittest'. A key part of this theory was that in the long run, the only species to survive were those that could adapt to their changing environment, have offspring and successfully pass on their genetic material from one generation to the next. Indeed adaptability is the core of Charles Darwin's theory on evolution.

In short, evolution is all about 'survival of the fittest'. On the surface this would appear to be true in the animal kingdom, where being the fastest, strongest or most agile is a major advantage.

For example, lions have strength, sharp teeth and the ability to run fast while elephants are big and intelligent. Snakes are venomous and cagey while whales are large and gentle. In each case, the animal in question has a physical attribute that enables them to survive and adapt to their particular environment.

> *In short, evolution is all about 'survival of the fittest'*

This adaptability is also evident in the human world but not at the physical level. Human beings seem relatively maladapted in terms of strength, speed and agility. Indeed, humans don't seem to have many attributes that give them physical domination over their environment. What they do have, however, is a very powerful psychology that is so adaptable it has allowed humans to survive to this day in great numbers.

There are Nine Survival Strategies Used to Survive in the Workplace

Within the powerful human psychology there are nine defences that we use to ensure our survival. These defences are built into our personalities, with each of us, depending on our personality type, automatically displaying a dominant psychological defence when faced with what we perceive to be a dangerous or threatening situation.

Now people will argue that there are other defences and this is true. The reason these nine psychological defences have been singled out is that time and time again they have delivered 'gold medal winning' performances where an individual, using one of these defences, has an excellent chance of surviving.

The First Survival Strategy

The first of these psychological defences focuses on following the rules. This means people using this defence to concentrate their attention on eliminating mistakes and being personally responsible. They feel 'righteous' about their personal responsibility and the perceived irresponsibility of other people. What they want is for everyone to be as aggressively compliant as they are.

The Second Survival Strategy

The second defence focuses on the ability to seduce others. These people seek to be cooperative and sensitive in order to elicit support from others – particularly those who are powerful. This strategy enables these people to get others to provide them with protection, food and support in return for their sensitivity and feelings of 'being connected'.

The Third Survival Strategy

The third defence focuses on completing tasks and appearing success-ful. These people concentrate all their energy on accomplishments and performance.

The Fourth Survival Strategy

The fourth defence is very similar to the second in that these people focus their attention on creating a connection between themselves and others. They do this because they believe the other person will provide them with large amounts of food, shelter, status and power in return for their perceived beauty as well as the fact that they are different, creative and unique.

The Fifth Survival Strategy

The fifth defence involves being rational, logical and analytical. These people are the tool-makers in primitive societies. They are the ones who saw the need for a tool, built that tool and then became experts in understanding how that tool worked. In today's modern world they are analysts and thinkers.

The Sixth Survival Strategy

The sixth defence involves looking out for the dangers that could be confronting the community or workplace. These are the people that can identify the threats and dangers to their safety and security and then warn everyone about them so that they can be prepared. In primitive and even modern environments they are the contrary questioners of the tribe.

The Seventh Survival Strategy

The seventh defence focuses on being clever, having bright ideas, being able to plan and seeing an optimistic future. These people also have the ability to take advantage of opportunities as they arise and develop multiple options in terms of what can be done and with whom in order for them to avoid being controlled or dominated by others.

The Eighth Survival Strategy

The eighth strategy is a simple one of taking power and control. These people need to be in charge. They have a patriarchal view of the world where they provide protection and strength in return for other people's loyalty and dependency.

The Ninth Survival Strategy

And finally the ninth psychological defence focuses upon unity. These people focus their attention on creating unity by establishing stability and harmony among all members of the tribe.

No Man or Woman is an Island

While each of us has our own inbuilt survival strategy, we do not live in a world of solitude. We are social animals whose survival strategies have developed not only as individuals but also across groups and tribes. Human beings, like all animals according to Charles Darwin, are focussed on their own personal survival until they discover that the odds of surviving are greatly increased when they become part of a tribe.

To become part of a tribe, however, we have to surrender a certain amount of our autonomy in order for us to fit in with our fellow tribes people. What this means is that we have to surrender some of our 'survival strategies' in order to take advantage of the increased 'defence' offered by being part of a tribe.

So, as you can see, human beings actually have two survival strategies. The first is to ensure our personal survival by relying on our own resources and ability to exert power and control over our environment. The second is our ability to interact with others in a tribal situation in order to increase the odds of our survival.

Survival versus High Performance

In primitive society, the odds of survival were further increased when all nine of the human psychological defences were represented and valued by a tribe. This is because each of the nine defences focuses on a different aspect of survival - from law and order, empathy, sensitivity, and accomplishment to identity, tools, strategy, opportunities, tribal strength, commitment and harmony.

In life, we too have to rely on other people to provide the remaining eight strategies needed to secure our existence. This means that today's most successful tribes are those with the adaptability of all nine survival strategies and whose leaders have evolved enough to encourage respect as well as diversity between warring families.

At work this may lead to survival but it will not lead to high performance.

The Lord of the Flies

In William Golding's novel, Lord of the Flies, a group of boys are marooned on an island in the South Pacific. As they begin to panic about their own survival they begin to return to their most primitive psychological state. Each of the characters adopts the strategy of complete autonomy to ensure their own survival at the expense of the others around them.

In this state of mind all others around them are considered to be either competitors or food. This is the most primitive form of survival where we try to ensure our own survival rather than the more advanced and adaptable method, namely ensuring our own survival within the context of our tribe.

Lord of the Flies explores the conundrum that without discipline, insight and awareness human beings descend into fighting for their own survival at the expense of the group. Ultimately this leads to their extinction because, ironically enough, survival can only be ensured by the very group we end up destroying.

The Physical Cost of Focusing on Survival in The Workplace

When we begin to focus on our survival at the expense of others, we establish the conditions necessary for the elimination of our own existence. While Lord of the Flies was written many years ago, the current plethora of 'reality' television programmes such as Survivor and Big Brother essentially explore the same issues

This is because these programmes are all about encouraging people to use their primitive strategies to survive. Perhaps that's why so many of us are drawn to watch these programmes - because we can see ourselves in the people on the screen and how they are behaving.

Indeed this voyeuristic enjoyment is much like the Romans watching the Christians dying in the Colosseum which was yet another example of human beings being reduced to the most primitive of instincts in order to try and ensure their own personal survival.

Maxamillian Kolby Demonstrated a Noble Alternative

This theory is again clearly demonstrated by the conditions in Auschwitz as described by Maxamillian Kolby. His book details how the Germans placed inmates of the concentration camp in bunkers with no food and water. They would then watch the 'spectacle' of these people tearing themselves apart, losing physical, psychological and spiritual control as they returned to their basest, most primitive ways of behaving.

Kolby volunteered to enter one of these bunkers in the place of another man and then convinced the others in the bunker to pray and begin to prepare themselves for death so they would die in a civilised and dignified manner. This so incensed the Nazis guards that they eventually injected Kolby with sulphuric acid in order to kill him.

> *In this state of mind all others around them are considered to be either competitors or food.*

These tragic events clearly illustrate that we, as individuals, have the ability to stop others and ourselves from descending into our most basic survival strategies. When this happens, individuals are perceived as heroes, saints and great leaders who are admired because they did not descend into the most primitive and base of behaviours in order to defend their own existence.

As human beings we have all experienced the desire to focus only on our own survival yet, in reality, deep down we all want to act with integrity, nobility and virtue in order to become full and complete human beings. The key to balancing these two desires is to unleash and then harness our survival instincts rather than letting them loose in an uncontrolled and habitual manner.

Could William Golding Write a Novel about Your Workplace?

So how different is today's corporate world compared to previous primitive societies or the fictional world of Lord of the Flies? We'd suggest not that different. Today's corporate world is just as much a 'jungle' made up of different families, religious groups and communities.

As part of that 'jungle', the moment we begin to panic about our own personal survival we spiral into the most primitive and least effective survival behaviours at the expense of whatever group, family or community we belong to.

Ironically, it's only when we're prepared to surrender our autonomy and selfish quest to protect only ourselves that our own survival becomes a much stronger possibility. It is also when most of the high-points of civilisation and human history have been achieved. This is because at our most base, human beings are only interested in their own survival and that of their offspring. Others are simply there to be exploited or eliminated.

At this point, human beings become possessed

by the passion for personal survival so much so that their behaviour becomes automatic or habitual. This passion is said to be blind to the essence of the human spirit, that is to be selfless and noble. When possessed by this passion we become habitual beings rather than human beings. In the case of Maxamillian Kolby, the surrender of personal survival transcended the baseness of human behaviour even at its most primitive.

Many Corporations Work Like Primitive Tribes

Many corporations I have worked with, although they may be more technically advanced, that is they have more sophisticated and developed tools, operate just like primitive tribes. And just like these primitive tribes they employ one of three primitive strategies.

The First Defensive Leadership Strategy

The first approach that leadership can take is to consider is to only employ people in their group that are the same as them. For all the members of the group this feels right because they all have the same survival strategy that seems to them to be sensible and logical.

Because everyone has the same survival strategy, they all get to hear what they perceive as being sensible ideas and solutions. Even their fears seem sensible. On the one hand this means the group will experience virtually no conflict but in reality it makes the group extremely vulnerable in terms of its ability to adapt to its environment. This is because the group has only one survival strategy and is missing the other eight.

The Second Defensive Leadership Strategy

The second approach is to ignore each other and try to win at each other's expense. This obviously feels good when we are winning

and bad when we lose. Here all the energy within the tribe or organisation goes into the politics of survival.

Leading the Team to Lift Their Defences

The third and most successful approach is to encourage all nine strategies to live together in harmony and mutual respect. This is what the essence of diversity is all about. The challenge is that for all of us, this plan is counter intuitive. This is because in seeking to encourage diversity to its maximum we must first surrender autonomy over our own survival.

Yet when we look back at our history, it is only when such diversity has been created that civilisation has flourished and tolerance within populations has been achieved.

The irony of all of this is that diversity and the bringing together of all nine survival strategies dramatically increases our potential for survival but, at the same time, it also increases the potential for conflict just as dramatically.

If everyone thought and acted the same way, there would be little if any conflict but people's ability to adapt to changing times becomes limited. In contrast, when there are nine different ways of thinking and behaving, the potential for conflict increases but so does the adaptability to respond positively to altered circumstances.

The more diverse a group the greater will be its range of skills, experience and flexibility. The less diverse a group, the more it has to rely on a single plan which it will rigidly repeat regardless of how its external environment may have changed. Diversity brings adaptability that, in turn, generates respect, tolerance, inclusion and civilisation.

If you look back at the history of the world, the

high points of civilisations have always been built on the philosophies of great leaders and enlightened heroes. These people are what the most powerful myths are based on.

Underlying the philosophies and actions of these leaders and heroes is always a platform that encourages diversity as well as a deep understanding of different points of view and the value these add to the wider group.

> *If you look back at the history of the world, the high points of civilisations have always been built on the philosophies of great leaders and enlightened heroes. These people are what the most powerful myths are based on.*

These enlightened leaders and heroes have always been prepared to surrender their own survival but the irony is that in doing so they knew that their surrender would actually help achieve what they were perceived as having given away – namely survival, not only of themselves but their tribe.

In the case of Australia, which is similar to the USA and Canada, many people consider this country to be a place of diversity, one that provides for all people who make Australia their home.

That is why, for so many Australians, the 2001 Tampa Crisis was so painful and unacceptable because in their view 'but for the Grace of God go I'. This is because many people in Australia consider themselves to be descended from refugees who now appear to be so unwelcome.

If you take this to a deeper, philosophical level, Australia's greatness and prosperity been built on migration and diversity that, in turn, has led

to brilliant creativity and social cohesion. What this clearly demonstrates is that when we are given the opportunity to allow other people to share in diversity it's beholden on us to do so. Advanced organisations have exactly the same approach and foundation.

Commercial Adaptability Equals Commercial Survival

In the commercial world, the ability of an organisation to beat other competitive tribes is directly related to its ability to access the right survival strategy for a particular situation. Corporations that have a diverse set of tools, perspectives and survival strategies are highly adaptive. As a consequence, when the environment that surrounds them changes they are able to move with the times.

A good example of commercial adaptability was the oil crisis of the 1970's. During this particular crisis, many organisations and businesses went to the wall because they were not able to adapt to the dramatically changed environment.

Those companies that did go under were unable to survive in a world of higher oil prices because they were fixated on only one or two survival strategies that proved to be inappropriate for the crisis they were facing. In contrast, those organisations that did survive did so because they had a balanced number of different survival strategies and as such were able to select the most appropriate strategy for the situation they were facing.

Your Survival Strategy Defines Your Core Belief/Neuro-Limbic Personality

As I said earlier, there are nine basic survival

strategies that organisations or communities use which have their genesis in human personality. Core Belief/Neuro-Limbic fixation is about individual survival not about optimum performance. When we become focused solely on our own personal survival, we hold on to our personalities passionately.

Even the most intelligent person secretly or unconsciously believes that their strategy for survival is the right one for the situation they're facing. It is only when we don't hold that position so passionately that we're able to see the position other people may have and thus alternative survival strategies that may be better suited to the current situation we're facing.

Your Passion is Your Pain

Let me give you an example of what we mean. Paul, the managing director of a leading consulting firm was working from home and suddenly his computer went dead, three hours before he was due to leave for the office to make a presentation to a potentially major client.

Faced with this situation, Paul quickly sought to identify the problem and solve it. In doing this he discovered that the power lead to the computer had been accidentally severed due to his desk resting on the cable. Paul's response was to rush down to his garage and grab a soldering iron in order to repair the cable.

Nearly one and half hours after he started trying to repair the cable, his son returned home and asked his father whether he had considered driving to the computer shop in the city to purchase a new power cable and thus solve the problem much more easily.

The return journey to the city would have taken approximately one hour and as such the

solution suggested by his son was obviously more logical and easily implemented. Paul, however, had missed this option completely because he was so passionately holding onto what he perceived to be the best 'survival strategy' for dealing with the situation.

Now this is only a microcosm of what is a macrocosm but if you were to apply this example to hundreds or thousands of situations that occur in an organisation then you'd be able to see that it's only when we let go of our passionately held positions that we're able to come up with more appropriate and effective solutions.

The Big Leadership Question

It is ironic that the word 'passionate' is used as a positive characteristic within organisations. It is true that a passion for survival is an extraordinary energy hence why we frequently describe human beings' fight for survival as extraordinary feats of endurance, strength and ingenuity.

The great issue for leaders is how to transform the passionate energy that we use to survive, but which is basically selfishly held, into a passion for the good of society or organisation and the survival of all within that society or organisation.

Only by unleashing the energy that goes into ensuring our own survival and using it to achieve a corporate endeavour that benefits everyone in the 'tribe', will communities and organisations become the best they can be. Powerful leaders have developed the ability to 'convert' the passion into nobility – this is at the core of transformational leadership.

Powerful leaders have the ability to 'convert' negative emotion and resistance into nobility.

Do we Create our own Suffering at Work?

The word passion comes from the Latin patior meaning to suffer. When we passionately hold on to our psychological positions we ultimately endanger our own survival. It is only when we surrender these passionately held positions that the chances of us surviving increases exponentially as does the survival chances of our 'tribe' or corporation.

Creativity, discretionary effort, synergistic teamwork and 'out-of-the-box' results only occur when all nine strategies for survival are acknowledged and embraced so that everybody within the tribe feels respected and included. This is because people within the tribe or corporation do not feel the need to fight to survive.

Rather these people are prepared to work cooperatively and synergistically for the common good because they feel respected and included. It is these feelings that allow them to observe and surrender their automatic or habitual primitive responses in favour of the higher functions of being human.

In contrast, if the inbuilt survival instincts of people are trigged, their passions come out of the box and they will fight will all their team or tribe members to ensure their own personal survival.

My Way or the Highway!

If the individuals in an organisation are focused on their own personal survival then that organisation is doomed. As an experienced consultant, much of my time has been spent working with and seeking to transform organisations where traditionally the leader has had one strategy, the senior management has a different one, middle management has a third strategy and some of the employees have another or there is a combination of all of the above.

Whatever the combination, everybody in the organisation, from the CEO through to the customer service person on the telephone or in the retail outlet, will genuinely believe they have the best strategy or solution to the problem or crisis the organisation is currently facing. As a result, each person will spend most of their time trying to convince everyone else in the organisation that they should adopt their particular strategy or solution.

They will do this because their passion comes from their fear and belief that everything will fall apart if their particular strategy or solution is not adopted. This is because each of us develops skills and abilities that enable us to successfully control our world.

Agreeing to see the world through another's eyes opens us up to the possibility that our survival skills may not be useful, sought after or valued. Rather than entertain the possibility that we may be redundant or powerless, we set about recreating our world so that our survival skills are guaranteed to be valuable and prestigious. In short, we create an illusionary need for our survival pathology.

The hardest task in such a situation is trying to convince us that there are other valid points of view other than our own. And the more passionate these debates become the more people feel as though they're not being listened to, not being respected and the less they're able to control what they say and do. Their thought processes and behaviours cease to be an inclusive exchange of possible solutions and rapidly descend into primeval habitual responses.

The moment the survival instinct takes over is when the focus of attention becomes winning the battle not the war. It is no longer about the vision of the organisation, corporate identity or immense potential of the people who comprise that organisation. Rather, the objectives of the organisation are thrown out the door and the members of the team turn on one another in a desperate effort to ensure their own survival. The result is that everyone inevitably goes down with the ship.

Perhaps the hardest task is trying to convince ourtselves that there are other valid points of view other than our own.

Our Corporate World can be as Primitive as a Jungle

Fascinatingly enough, as leaders and managers we can see so many of the childlike behaviours that others display but cannot see these same responses in ourselves. Indeed itís always amazing to see how childlike or primitive our colleagues and employees can behave in meetings, negotiations, client discussions or even at parties.

But funnily enough, it's always other people that seem to get stressed, upset or angry in such a ridiculous way and never ourselves. This is caused by two psychological impacts of personality engagement.

The first sees the focus of our attention directed outward to where the threat to our survival can be found. This perceived threat heightens our senses and, as a result of this intensified attention, other people's behaviour becomes our focus.

Secondly, as our attention is directed out it becomes easier to observe the behaviour of

others but almost impossible to observe it in ourselves. This is because when our passion for survival is aroused and our Core Belief/Neuro-Limbic fixation is engaged all ability to self-observe ceases.

Our Blind Spot can be Blinding to Others

I sometimes have a conversation at home with my partner where I am alerted of one of my annoying foibles. I sincerely argue in this situation that the person they are describing is nothing like me! The reason these discussions happen is because often enough my ability to self-observe is turned off. And what is worse, as I become more stressed I passionately hold on to my survival strategy and begin to exaggerate the behaviours of my other half in order to defend my own position.

The rule here is that when we passionately hold onto our survival strategies as a result of our Core Belief/Neuro-Limbic Types being in full operation, all our abilities of self-observation stop. This is because when this part of our Core Belief/Neuro-Limbic fixation is fully engaged we become solely focused on survival and are unable to learn anything or demonstrate any kind of flexibility.

The result is that we repeat a set of strategies of survival that are a million years old, strategies that have been repeated for generation after generation. In fact, in this state we are no more creative than our forebears a thousand generations ago who used identical strategies to fight off the mammoths in the great Savannas of Central Europe.

How Entrenched In Core Beliefs/Neuro-Limbic Types is your Workforce?

In an organisation where 75 per cent of the people at any one time are entrenched in their Core Belief/Neuro-Limbic fixation there will be some very obvious symptoms. Firstly, such an organisation will have a hard time changing because it will be entrenched in its ways.

Secondly, the actual goals and corporate objectives of the organisation will have become lost. This is because the organisation's employees will be focusing on their own survival or personal gratification rather than the aims and objectives of the corporate entity.

That is why every 10 or 15 years organisations have to ask themselves what is their reason for being there? What are they trying to achieve? Where are they going? How are they going to get there?

Culture is a Function of Core Belief / Neuro-Limbic fixation

In today's corporate environment, culture is defined as the sum total of the survival types present in an organisation. If an organisation has a large number of one type the focus of that organisation will be directed towards a certain aspect of survival. And this brings us to the second psychological impact of our survival strategies – the energy that follows attention.

> *Organisations with a low representation of a particular survival type and thus survival instinct will have major blind spots in terms of its strategic survival.*

In the case of an organisation where its attention is focused on a particular aspect of survival, the energy, resources, time and money of that organisation will also be directed to that same aspect of survival. This is because the chosen strategic direction of that organisation will not be based on what

that organisation wants needs to adapt to its changing environment.

Rather it will be based on satisfying the psychological survival needs of the most represented Core Belief/Neuro-Limbic types present in that organisation. This 'over-representation' of a type will create 'group think' and inflexibility.

In reverse, the impact is just as damaging. Organisations with a low representation of a particular survival type and thus survival instinct will have major blind spots in terms of its strategic survival.

Obviously experience tells us that some industries or professions are going to be over-represented with some types and under-represented in others. The point here is that successful organisations do not seek to change the composition of their Core Belief/Neuro-Limbic types. Indeed in many countries such actions would be illegal.

Organisations cannot simply sack large numbers of people because they are perceived as having the wrong type. Certainly, at worst, it would be unethical for organisations to use this approach to re-engineer the mix of types. The message here is not for organisations to seek to change the composition of types but rather to be aware that blind spots exist and then seek to understand the alternative survival strategies that are available.

The objective is not to use a person's Core Belief/Neuro-Limbic type to select, promote or move them within an organisation. Rather, the objective is to encourage everyone in the organisation to act creatively and step 'outside of their comfort zone'. In a nutshell, the objective is literally to bring sight to the blind.

In Australia, the Queensland police force

used personality typing for a number of years to select the best personality types to fit into a culture of service. At some point in this process it was discovered, during the Fitzgerald Commission of Inquiry, that the culture for which people were being selected was corrupt.

As a result of this corruption, some of the most senior people in that force were asked to retire but this approach did not solve the entrenched problems within the force. This was because the people responsible for recruiting new police offices had, by habit and because of their need to 'survive', selected people who were the same personality type as thus had the same flaws.

To resolve this problem, a whole new recruitment process was introduced. The police training methodology was put under a microscope and the focus shifted to include recruiting police officers from areas outside the State. People were chosen because of their different demographics. Notably, more women and older police officers were chosen who, it was felt, would have stronger characters and personalities to cope with a culture of service.

A Culture of Analysis Paralysis

In 2002, in my role as a consultant I was appointed to work with a large transport company based in Australia that was over represented with strategic thinkers – that is analytical problem finders and solvers.

As a result of this over-representation, I discovered that the organisation was beset by an inability to make decisions as demonstrated by the company's large and growing number of bureaucratic processes, all of which had been put in place by these strategic thinkers to protect them from ever having to make a decision.

Through our ongoing research I also discovered that the company was beset by problem of priesthoods, that is where intellectual or technical expertise was the criteria upon which people were promoted to management positions.

These problems were caused by the over-representation of not one but two Core Belief/Neuro-Limbic types. Such a situation clearly demonstrates how certain Core Belief/Neuro-Limbic types can impact the focus of attention within an organisation. Just as our Core Belief/Neuro-Limbic fixation dictates where we focus our attention, so the mix of types within a company will govern where the collective attention of an organisation will be focused.

Money and Energy Follows Core Beliefs

On an individual level, money and energy follows where we focus our attention. The same is true for organisations that have an over- representation of certain Core Belief/Neuro-Limbic types.

Because of the dominance of one or two types, an organisation's focus of attention will be on certain aspects that are aligned with the survival strategies of the over-represented type. The result will be that all of the organisation's resources will tend to be channelled into funding these people's particular obsession.

This expenditure will happen regardless of whether it's right for the organisation's current markets, customers, is regarded as best practice or will help achieve specific short or long-term corporate objectives. This is because when people move into survival mode they become locked into their blind passion.

You Can't Manage What You Can't Measure

Professors Turner and Crawford, as described in their book Change Power, conducted an Australia-wide study of organisations that we going through the process of change. As part of their research, they analysed those organisations that had managed to navigate their way through change successfully.

They also identified self-observation as being the most important leadership capability within those organisations that had successfully coped with change. Self-observation was defined as an ability to see what you, as a leader, is doing and then being able to monitor this behaviour.

Only when they could change their leader's underlying assumptions would they be able to start changing the underlying assumptions of the culture.

Similarly, in his books on emotional intelligence, Daniel Goleman identified the need for leaders to be able to see their own Core Belief/Neuro-Limbic fixation and inherent habitual passions and then seek to manage these passions, not just in themselves but also in others.

The Role of Leadership

The role of true leadership is to convert the energy of individuals from their own personal survival to the performance of the team. That is why leadership is all about the ability of an individual to transform the primitive energy of survival that we all have into a more noble, elegant and graceful energy that is designed to serve the common good.

Leadership is also about being able to make sure that when you become entrenched in your own survival type and feel yourself beginning to passionately focus on ensuring your own survival, you're able to step back, observe what you're starting to feel and do and then

change your behaviour to ensure you don't trigger the same 'survival' instinct in everyone else around you.

Peter Senge in his book The Fifth Discipline which, when it was first published, caused a revolution in how learning organisations were perceived, wrote:

'Managers must learn to reflect on their current mental models, that is their primitive survival strategy, until prevailing assumptions are brought into the open, there is no reason to expect mental models, that is, culture and personality to change, and there is little purpose in systems-wide thinking. If managers believe, that is passionately hold their world views, and believe they are facts rather than a set of assumptions, then they will not be open to challenging their world views'.

Peter Senge argued that human beings needed to be able to self-observe. This, he argued, would enable them to see the underlying assumptions, agendas and motivations that dictated and drove how they behaved. He also argued that human beings needed to explain and discuss their behaviours with others. Only when they had observed and discussed their behaviours with a certain degree of detachment from their passionate beliefs would they be in a position to try and change their underlying assumptions.

This, he argued, was also the case for leaders. Only when they could change their own underlying assumptions would they able to start changing the underlying assumptions of their organisation.

Based on Peter Senge's findings and theories, the question we need to ask ourselves is 'are organisations driven by personal survival or by a surrender of that survival in favour of the aims and objectives of the organisation?'

Senge's Four Pillars of Leadership

Peter Senge, in his book The Fifth Discipline, also argues that there are four key pillars on which leadership is based. The first of these pillars is 'Personal Mastery', that is self-discipline. Peter Senge believed that personal mastery is the very skill we need to manage ourselves as adults rather than children.

For example, there is an interesting story where children were given the choice of taking one lolly now or two lollies in two hours. Twenty years later these same children were measured to see how successfully they had negotiated childhood and adolescence. In almost every case, the child who accepted two lollies two hours later seemed to have done better than the ones who, because they were unable to discipline themselves, took the one lolly up front. As you can see, personal mastery is a set of very advanced skills that human beings need to use to ensure they behave like adults rather than 'react compulsively'. This is describing appropriate behaviour rather than compulsive behaviour.

The second pillar of leadership identified by Peter Senge is 'Shared Vision', that is an organisation's ability to have all its members move in the same direction. This ability requires people to surrender their own direction, the one in which they are driven to go by their need to survive, in favour of a corporate vision. This corporate vision is not someone else's vision but rather a vision that has been negotiated and developed Through discussion and a contribution from all the members of the corporation or team.

Peter Senge's third pillar is 'Team Leading'. This refers to those strategies we all learnt in the sand-pit in kindergarten where we didn't just play with a small red toy but were able to share this toy with other people. These strategies were all about us learning how to use tools, do things and master certain situations by learning from the team. During this process, we would discover that we could learn from others rather than having to learn everything by ourselves.

> *Personal mastery is a set of very advanced skills that human beings need to use to ensure they behave like adults rather than 'react compulsively'.*

The final and most important pillar of Peter Senge's theory of leadership is the identification and management of mental models, that is what we call Core Belief/Neuro-Limbic fixation types. According to Peter Senge:

'One thing all managers know is that many of the best ideas never get put into practice, that brilliant strategies fail to get translated into action and that systemic insights never find their way into operating policies.'

Certainly the many years of research we have conducted with organisations throughout the world would appear to support Peter Senge's view. Time and time again we have found that managers in organisations aren't there to sabotage the organisation. Rather they want to be part of an organisation that uplifts them.

They don't want to be part of an organisation where, on a daily basis, they have to engage their survival strategies and are thus threatened to a point where they must use the basest and most primitive aspects of their personalities to ensure their own personal survival. What we have found is that managers go to work wanting to be creative, hoping that their day will be an ennobling experience. According to

Peter Senge:

'We've come to believe this failure comes, not from weak intentions, wavering will or even non-systemic understanding but from mental models, that is personality. More specifically, new insights fail to get into practice because they conflict with deeply held, that is primitive internal images of how the world works. Images that limit us to the habitual and familiar ways of thinking and acting, that is why the discipline of managing mental models, that is personality, promises to be the major breakthrough in building learning organisations'.

This insight by Peter Senge is particularly interesting because what he is saying is that it's only through the management of Core Belief/Neuro-Limbic fixation that we're able to get to the very centre of managing complex modern organisations. Only by managing our Core Belief/Neuro-Limbic fixation will the other great pillars of shared vision, team learning and personal mastery actually take place. And it's only when we've identified our deeply held primitive ways of seeing the world will we be able to effectively manage our Core Belief/Neuro-Limbic fixation type.

What's also interesting about Peter Senge's observations is that 15 years ago, when he first wrote his book, the breakthrough in managing Core Belief/Neuro-Limbic fixation type had not yet been attained. We would argue that no Core Belief/Neuro-Limbic fixation typing system, until now, has been powerful enough to be used in such a way that it forms a key part of the strategic management of human resources within an organisation. That is why the learning organisation movement has floundered - because they had not been able to find the holy grail of managing Core Belief/Neuro-Limbic fixation.

Based on my own experience and research, I believe there are three stages of leadership practice, the first of which is 'Self Observation and Management', that is knowing your own Core Belief/Neuro-Limbic type and breaking your habitual focus of attention.

If you're to develop this ability, you need to know what triggers your Core Belief/Neuro-Limbic fixation and habitual responses. You need to know what actually sets your inherent survival strategy in motion? Of course this is going to vary from person-to-person and will depend, to some degree, on your life experiences. There is, however, a strong correlation between what triggers people's survival strategies and their personalities.

Once you master self observation and understand the relationship between your Core Belief/Neuro-Limbic fixation and what triggers your survival strategy, the task then is to transform your passion from focusing on 'personal survival' to focusing on 'the objectives of the Team and the team's overall performance'. This is what many of the great mystical writers have called 'transforming lead into gold', the process of alchemy.

The second stage of leadership practice is understanding the passions and how you can ride rather than slay the dragon. It's certainly interesting to look at how the West and the East have dealt with the issue of the very magical dragon, a creature that is beyond human control, which has the potential to do great good as well as evil.

When a person moves into 'survival mode' they will trigger the same primitive survival instinct in everyone around them.

In the East, the focus is on riding the dragon to prosperity and abundance. In the West the focus is on slaying the dragon, bringing the dragon under control and mercilessly driving it into the dust.

In terms of our passions, it's also about riding or slaying the dragon. If we seek to slay the dragon we will try and suppress our passions. The result will be that our organisation will become sterile and bland. If we seek to ride the dragon, we will learn to control our passions and thus empower ourselves and other people to transform our passion for survival into a more ennobling and creative passion of organisational focus and direction.

Waves and Ripples Of Dysfunction

Another important thing to remember about our passions is that they move through an oganisation in waves and ripples. When a person moves into 'survival mode' they will trigger the same primitive survival instinct in everyone around them. The end result is that as each person enters into the process of survival they will trigger the next person and so on until the whole organisation becomes transfixed on a rather pathetic and sad quest for personal survival rather than the journey towards organisational performance, success and nobility.

As this 'survival mode' moves through an organisation like a great wave people will, at this point, misunderstand what is happening. Often they will think that somebody is actually furious whereas, in reality, they have simply gone into survival mode and, because of their particular type, will be reacting angrily, a response that will then trigger the survival mode in everyone around them. This does not mean, however, that the response, as everyone moves into survival mode, will be the same.

Each type has its own special range of passions or emotions that are linked to them entering into survival mode. Some people might get angry while others may feel extremely anxious, depressed or sad. Only when an organisation has people all with the same type will the reaction to entering 'survival mode' be the same.

This is why the military forces often encounter difficulties when it comes to managing and understanding their people. Often, senior officers will stand at the front of a room and bark out orders to people of different ranks and, more importantly, different types.

The key is not to let people simply unleash their passions as a result of their survival instincts.

The result will be a whole range of different pathological responses that, like a wave, will take the group of people in that room in a whole range of different emotional directions that are completely uncontrollable.

Now we're not saying that people's passions are a bad thing. What we're saying is that the key is not to let people simply unleash their passions as a result of their survival instincts having been triggered. Rather, the aim is to unleash and then manage these passions so they are transformed into a more useful and effective source of energy.

In achieving this, the role of leaders is to lead by example. When faced by a huge wave of passions as people move into survival mode and trigger this same instinct in the people around them, leaders need to focus on holding on to the essential nobility of the human being by not giving in to their own passions and need for personal survival.

Only by resisting the urge and passions people feel when they are in survival mode, will a leader be able to halt the full force of the tidal wave as it moves through an organisation, country, or even family. And the only way leaders will be able to do this successfully is to develop self-observation, the first pillar of leadership practice.

Historically, the response from most leaders when faced with a tidal wave of passions and people focused on personal survival has been to either ignore them or respond with their own survival strategy.

Certainly, it's interesting that politicians, advertising gurus or others seeking to manipulate the emotions of people usually end up triggering their own survival strategies in order to get the response they want from the very people they are seeking to influence.

Of course, the irony is that once people are locked into their survival strategy their responses can be predicted to a very high degree of accuracy. Indeed in recent years there have been a number of studies where the correlation between types and their response when in survival mode have been as high as 90 per cent.

For some leaders this ability to predict people's behaviour can be very dispiriting as they watch teams, organisations or even whole populations of human beings resort to the most base and primitive emotions and behaviours rather than the more noble and virtuous aspects of human essence to which we can all aspire.

That is why the third stage of leadership practice is being able to understand people's passions. As human beings all of us have three cardinal emotions - anger, fear and disapproval. A key part of effective leadership is to identify which passion is displayed and why and how you,

as a leader, can administer an antidote so people's fight for survival is transformed into a fight for compassion, goodness, creativity and productivity.

As well as the three stages of leadership practice, there are two vitally important laws that impact how effective leaders are in their quest to behave nobly and for the common good.

The first of these is the Law of Countervailing Forces. The second is the Law of Transformation. In my experience, having worked with some of Australia's largest organisaations, the leaders who not only understand, but also apply these laws achieve the employee engagement and discretionary effort required to deliver on their strategic plan. Part science, part artform – this is the essence of true leadership.

The Historical Underpinnings of Transformational Leadership

Many Westerners who first studied Transformational Leadership believed that it was the work of the 20th Century philosopher and psychologist Giorgio Gurdjieff. In actual fact the foundations of transformation leadership can be traced back to the writings of the monk Evagrias Epontis who, writing in the 3rd Century A.D, was part of the movement towards contemplative existence in the old Byzantine Empire.

Ancient Insight – Modern Application

Evagrias was an outstanding researcher and scholar of his day. He was a brilliant writer and a great observer of human behaviour. His main interests were in contemplative proto-psychology, namely how human beings behaved when they were put under the intense discipline of contemplative practice.

He wanted to know what happened to humans

when they were required to fast or do without human contact or forced to work long hours or all of these conditions. At the time of his writings, the monastic community was like a large theoretical laboratory involving over 150,000 people. Back then, in the 3rd Century, they developed an extraordinary oral perdition that pieced together all the information documented by Evagrias about the psychology of human beings in closed monastic communities.

Evagrias was the first to catalogue the passions described in the transformation process. Indeed he wrote extensively about these passions, how they were formed, how they affected people's behaviour and relationships, the physiological characteristics different people displayed and how their passions affected communities as a whole. And it was on these works that the investigation into personalities in both the East and West were based and indeed endured over the past 17 hundred years.

In the East, Evagrias' teachings were embraced and further developed by the secret brotherhoods of the Sufis, the mystical arm of Islam. In contrast, in the West Evagrias' teachings were carried on by the mystical writers of theology in Christianity and Judaism, with the latter writing specifically about aspects of the Kamala.

Much of these writings were either lost or declared dangerous and heretical. Many years later, some of these writings were discovered in various libraries around the world by a late 19th Century movement called the Occidental Movement which, at the time, was immensely influential thanks to followers such as Karl Jung and Sigmund Freud. This Occidental Movement began to search out and gather these texts from the mystical traditions of both East and West. They then began to develop their own insights and theories on which the

psychoanalytical movement and writings of Karl Jung are strongly based.

The Transformation Process

In 1950, Oscar Ichazo discovered the transformation process and decided to split it into two parts. The first of these was the part that deals with human typology. The result of this split was that in the 1980s, in defence of his writings, Oscar Ichazo sued one of the leading researchers and authors on human typology, Helen Palmer.

In the USA courts, Oscar Ichazo argued that he had been given information about the transformation process by the archangel Metatron. As you can imagine this did not sit well with the US legal system, the result being that the judge presiding over the case ended up ruling that in the USA, because there is a clear separation between the Church and State, he was not legally able to comment on the copyright of Metatron's vision.

The second part of transformation process, based on the division by Oscar Ichazo, was the process of emotional conversion as described by Bennet, one of Giorgio Gurdjieff's most brilliant students. This part describes the nature of cycles.

Both Oscar Ichazo and Bennet separated the human personality from the cycle of transformation thus fragmenting the general theory of transformation, a division that continues today.

In 1995 Stanford University started the process of clinically validating the types. This gave rise to the Stanford Inventory. Professor David Daniels, from Stanford, also worked closely with David Burke to explore how personality and transformation could be used in the workplace.

This information was extensively trialed and refined in the Australian corporate sector by Burow and Asscoiates from 1996 until 2003 and the findings were summarised in a groundbreaking book by Peter Burow and David Burke in 2004: Transforming Organisations: The Steps to Creating a High Performance Culture.

Since then, 30 senior organisational change practitioners have been certified in Transformational Leadership by Burow and Burke in Australia, the US and Brazil.

Today, national/international organisations using the framework include:

- Australian Red Cross Blood Service (Aus)
- Brisbane City Council (Qld Aus)
- Central Intelligence Agency (USA)
- Cincinnati Reds (USA)
- Crèche and Kindergarten Association Department of Primary Industries (Qld Aus)
- Forrest Products Commission (WA Aus)
- Great Barrier Reef Park Marine Authority (Qld Aus)
- Mandura City Council (WA Aus)
- Peel Development Commission (WA Aus)
- Qld Chamber of Commerce & Industry UNICEF (USA)
- US Postal Service (USA)
- Corporate
- Ariat (USA)
- Boeing (USA)
- Cara Operations (Canada)
- CISCO Systems (USA)
- Deutsche Bank (Aus)
- Disney (USA)
- General Motors (USA)
- Hewlett Packard (USA)
- Hyatt (USA)
- Kimpton Hotel Chain (USA)
- Kip McGrath Coaching (Aus)
- KLM (USA)
- Kodak (USA)
- Lucent Technologies (USA)
- Mark Lynch Pty Ltd (AUS)
- Marriott (USA)
- Motorola (USA)
- People Soft (USA)
- Phillips Electronics (USA)
- PricewaterhouseCoopers (Aus)
- Proctor & Gamble (USA)
- Prudential (USA)
- Reebok (USA)
- Shell (USA)
- Silicon Graphics (USA)
- Sony (USA)
- Sun Microsystems (USA)

- Toyota (USA)
- United Customer Management Services (Aus)
- VLSI Technology (USA)
- Woolworths (Aus)
- World Travel BTI (USA)
- Xerox (USA)

The framework has also been used in the following settings:

- International planning meetings
- Board rooms
- Executive groups of large corporations
- Middle management
- Shop floors
- Marriage guidance settings
- Women's groups

And has been used for a range of purposes including:

- Diagnosis
- Planning
- Facilitation, Facilitation design
- Mapping conversations
- Coaching
- Integrating and clarifying issues
- Galvanising and coalescing shared will

The Three Parts of Transformational Leadership

The general theory of the transformation has three distinct parts. The first part is the theory of human typology and the part people's passions play in the development of their sense of self.

The second part of the general theory of transformation involves the cycle of transformation where people move from their survival strategy to a position of heroic nobility and extraordinary creativity where falling in love is the central aspect or focus of the person or organisation.

The third part of transformational leadership involves the issue of countervailing forces; that is how people, in seeking to implement their survival strategies, end up creating the very perception or belief that they're seeking to defend themselves against. When you combine these three aspects, the general transformation theory becomes an extraordinarily powerful and rich description of human behaviour and transformation.

The Power of Transformational Leadership

Transformational leadership was designed to be used as an integrated model. By understanding people's Core Belief/Neuro-Limbic type, transformational leadership can be used to identify the emotional fixation while the transformation process can be used to release people from this 'fixation' or their habitual pattern of behaviour when in survival mode. Transformational leadership was designed to be liberating, that is to release people from their habitual survival strategies by putting them in touch with the most divine and noble aspects of human essence, namely all that is great about human beings.

> *Our inability to manage our own emotions or even observe ourselves precludes us from ever being able to observe or manage other people.*

By putting people in touch with these aspects, they are then able to fulfil their potential as human beings. In a nutshell, transformational leadership is a model that describes both the personal obstacles and pathways or processes towards human enlightenment.

When the Occidental Movement, back in the 1950s, split transformational leadership, they removed the redeeming power of the model. They did this by encouraging their followers to celebrate rather than transcend their primitive habitual personality, thus destroying the real value of the transformation process.

The purpose of my organisational transformation consulting practice has been to reunite the three elements of the transformation model – that is the Law of Countervailing Forces, the Cycle of Transformation and Habitual Personality (Core Beliefs/Neuro-limbic types).

The reason for wanting to integrate the three elements is simple. The integrated model is unique because it works at both an individual and social/organisational level. Amazingly, the insights we gain and methods we use at an individual level can also be applied at a social or organisational level .

Indeed, one of the rules we used in seeking to understand the work we do is that the microcosm is the macrocosm. By understanding the small you can actually understand the large. In understanding the personal you can understand the corporate or cosmic. What this also means, however, is that personal blindness leads to macro blindness. An inability to understand our own motivation leads to an inability to understand others. Similarly, our inability to manage our own emotions or even observe ourselves precludes us from ever being able to observe or manage other people or an organisation as a whole.

And so personal psychology becomes organisational psychology and the cycle of transformation, as outlined by the general theory of transformational leadership, seeks to release individual creativity, freedom and energy at both a personal and organisational level.

Over the past two decades, I have worked with all kinds of organisations. The majority of these organisations have argued that they have a developed or long-established culture, one that is a key factor in their success. In reality, many of these organisations had fragmented cultures as result of the many teams that operate within the organisation, teams that seek to influence not only their own members but other teams as well. Sometimes these teams have a positive influence on the organisation, other times they have a negative influence. It all depends on whether the leader of the team consciously or unconsciously takes his or her people through the cycle of transformation.

According to the theory of transformational leadership, the cycle of transformation happens naturally. It is one of the laws of nature which people don't have to invent because it happens all the time. The only reason it doesn't successfully occur every time is because people's survival strategies stand in its way.

This means that if people, as members of a team or organisation, were freed from their survival strategies they would be able to transcended their most base and primitive behaviours and passions. The result would be organisations that are highly adaptive, creative, energetic and passionate, all of which are hallmarks of a positive culture.

The role of leaders, in the Transformation process, is to look at the cycle, identify what is coming up, see how many in the organisation, team or group will get stuck at which point depending on their personality type, and then identify what needs to be done to move these people on to the next stage so the organisation can successfully complete the transformation cycle.

This is the philosophers' stone of organisational change, the tribal leadership of turning lead into synergistic gold. If the process is applied well, it is the ultimate application of ancient wisdom in a modern context. This is because fundamentally our survival strategies have not changed over thousands of years. As such, we look identical to our forebears back on the plains of Africa when in survival mode. Think back to some of the meetings you have attended and some of the things that have been said, the reactions and body language of the people in the room. For most of us, what we see makes perfect sense because we can almost see the plains of Africa as the ideal background for some of the meetings we have held.

Recommended Reading

1. Kotter, John P, *Leading Change*. Harvard Business School Press, Boston, 1996.

2. Scholtes, Peter R, Joiner, Brian L, and Streibel, Barbara J, *The Team Handbook*. 2nd Edition. Oriel Inc, 1996.

3. Turner, Dennis, and Crawford, Michael, Change Power: Capabilities That Drive Corporate Renewal. Business and Professional Publishing, 1998.

4. Loehr, J, and Schwartz, T, *The Power of Full Engagement*. Allen & Unwin, 2003.

5. Gilson, C, Pratt, M, Roberts, K, and Weymes, E, *Peak Performance*. HarperCollins Publishers, 2000.

6. Stoltz, P, "Response Ability", in *Business: The Ultimate Resource*. Bloomsbury Publishing, 2002.

7. King, C (ed), *Manager's Handbook*. Dorling Kindersley Limited, 2002.

8. Peters, T, *Liberation Management*. Alfred A Knopf, Inc, NY, 1992.

9. Fritz, R, *Corporate Tides*. Butterworth-Heinemann Ltd, 1994.

10. Flanagan, N and Finger, J, Just About Everything A Manager Needs To Know. Blum Press, Brisbane, Australia, 1998.

11. Martin, D, *TeamThink: Using The Sports Connection To Develop, Motivate, And Manage A Winning Business Team*. Penguin Books USA Inc, 1993.

12. Finlayson, A, *Questions that Work*. AMACOM Books, NY, 2001.

13. Tichy, N M, and Sherman, S, *Control your Destiny or Someone Else Will*. Doubleday, NY, 1993.

14. Quinn, J B, Intelligent Enterprise. The Free Press, NY, 1992.

About the Author

Peter Burow specialises in employee engagement, cultural development and leadership development.

His understanding of the emotional and cognitive impact of change on the individual and the neuroscience of how we resist change make him a valued advisor to leaders in both the private sector and government alike.

Peter's client list includes some of Australia's largest and best-known corporates including PricewaterhouseCoopers, AMP and BHP Billiton and a broad range of government departments and instrumentalities at both a State and Federal level.

He is the author of several books on the subject of leadership development and organisational transformation.

www.ingramcontent.com/pod-product-compliance
Lightning Source LLC
Chambersburg PA
CBHW081540220326
41598CB00036B/6500